Incredible Edible Science

Incredible Edible Science

Recipes for Developing Science and Literacy Skills

Liz Plaster and Rick Krustchinsky

Redleaf Press®
www.redleafpress.org
800-423-8309

Published by Redleaf Press
10 Yorkton Court
St. Paul, MN 55117
www.redleafpress.org

First edition 2010
Cover design by Erin New
Interior typeset in Adobe Chaparral and designed by Percolator
Photo on page 164 courtesy of Liz Plaster
Illustrations on pages 231 through 234 courtesy of Claire Schipke.
Printed in the United States of America
18 17 16 15 14 13 12 11 2 3 4 5 6 7 8 9

Library of Congress Cataloging-in-Publication Data
Plaster, Liz.
Incredible edible science : recipes for developing science and literacy skills / by Liz Plaster and Rick Krustchinsky. – 1st ed.
p. cm.
Includes bibliographical references.
ISBN 978-1-60554-017-7 (alk. paper)
1. Science–Study and teaching (Early childhood)–Activity programs. 2. Language arts (Early childhood)–Activity programs. 3. Food–Study and teaching (Early childhood)–Activity programs. 4. Cookery–Study and teaching (Early childhood)–Activity programs. I. Krustchinsky, Rick. II. Title.
LB1139.5.S35P6 2010
372.3'5–dc22

2009026431

Printed on FSC®-certified paper

Dedicated to my family:
Your willingness and loving acceptance in your role as research subjects for my "cooking" continues to inspire and encourage me to keep learning and exploring. Dad, thanks for teaching me how to "fly." Bob, thanks for being the wind beneath my wings.

And to my colleagues and students:
Thank you for the support, laughter, challenges, and inspiration you have provided me.
My life is better having been touched by each of you.

Liz Plaster

Dedicated to my wife and children:
Your love and support over the years has helped me to be better than I could ever have been without it. You were always merry and excited and ready for my next adventure.

And to the thousands of students that have been in my classes over the past thirty years:
You have inspired me to continually want to grow and develop as an educator. Thank you for teaching me more about life and the education profession than I could ever teach you.

Rick Krustchinsky

CONTENTS

OBSERVING/SMELL ACTIVITIES

OBSERVING/TASTE ACTIVITIES

OBSERVING/TOUCH ACTIVITIES

OBSERVING/SOUND ACTIVITIES

CLASSIFYING ACTIVITIES

COMMUNICATING ACTIVITIES

MEASURING ACTIVITIES

INFERRING ACTIVITIES

PREDICTING ACTIVITIES

Chapter 4
Blending Language and Literacy into Science Activities

SCIENCE/LITERACY ACTIVITIES

ACKNOWLEDGMENTS

We are reluctant to single out people specifically, noting how many people in our lives made this book possible, yet we had specific assistance from several people. We are grateful to the people at Redleaf Press who saw the vision for our book ideas and helped turn them into a reality. Each of you at Redleaf Press was very kind throughout the writing process and made the writing of this book fun and exciting. We would like to thank Karen Vanek, Rebecca Sheinberg, and Scott Wille for their help and suggestions in reviewing the manuscript.

Special thanks to all those who worked collaboratively to turn their knowledge into action, creating more effective early childhood programs during this last decade. Though there are many more who could be listed, a few that cannot go unmentioned are Dr. Al Tarlov, Dr. Susan Landry, Dr. Nita Copely, Evelyn Moore, Kaitlin Guthrow, Kara Johnson, Pam Schiller, Frances Schneider, Suzanne Hinds, Carol Shattuck, and Scott Wille. Their experiences inspired the creation of the science-literacy connection in this book.

INTRODUCTION

Incredible Edible Science: Recipes for Developing Science and Literacy Skills is designed to provide a menu of meaningful cooking experiences and food investigations for early childhood educators and the children they teach. The book emphasizes the need for educators like you to nurture the inquisitive minds of young children through the use of food-related and cooking activities. This book, like a cookbook, has recipes that incorporate activities about food and cooking, teaching children, and the nature of science.

Chapter 1, Food for Thought, provides an overview of background information and educational theory in early childhood education relating to current brain research, science and young children, the language and literacy connection, and social development.

Chapter 2, Setting the Table for Learning, helps you get organized for teaching the chapter 3 and 4 activities, which cover communication, safety and health, materials and equipment, snack centers, and the role of the teacher.

Chapter 3, Cooking Up Basic Science Process Skills, emphasizes the importance of basic science process skills in learning science concepts and vocabulary. Food-related activities organized into six categories—observing, classifying, communicating, measuring, inferring, and predicting—help develop basic science process skills. Each activity also subtly introduces a literacy element in the Words You Can Use vocabulary list. The What You Need section lists required materials, while the What You Do section takes you through the activity step by step. Each lesson also includes Questions You Can Ask, with suggestions for questions you can pose to the children throughout the activity to ensure their interaction and learning.

Chapter 4, Blending Language and Literacy into Science Activities, provides teachers with science activities that feature all the elements of the chapter 3 activities and also incorporate three language and literacy components:

- Sound Play: phonological-awareness activities, including tongue twisters, poems, rhymes, songs, and fingerplays
- Reading Experience: a list of suggested books related to the activity
- More You Can Try: a list of suggestions for varying or extending the activity to tailor it to the children in your care

Each investigation in *Incredible Edible Science* is packed with detail and excitement and is explained in clear, succinct fashion. The investigations require simple, inexpensive materials easily found in your classroom, care center, home, or neighborhood.

We envision this book to be used by teachers of young children ages three to eight years, in a variety of settings, including public or private prekindergarten, kindergarten, first and second grade and Head Start programs, and by university professors for teacher training programs. Families and homeschoolers will also find it a rich source of science ideas for their own children.

Food for Thought

Food has a very special place in people's lives. Eating with others makes food part of a wonderful, exciting, and sharing experience. This is particularly true for young children. They love to eat—at least most of the time! Food is necessary for nutritional reasons, and eating with others provides opportunities for fun and socialization. Eating is done at home, school, work, in restaurants, and at birthday parties, family gatherings, or other celebrations.

In many school settings, food is often served family style so children can learn about table manners, proper nutrition, and food preparation, and can participate in appropriate mealtime interactions. Given families' busy lifestyles, as well as the convenience of fast-food restaurants, these mealtime and food-preparation activities in the classroom may provide one of the few opportunities for children to engage in this social interaction centered on a daily routine.

According to Alfving et al., "As one of man's primary needs, food has been referred to in literature, music, legends, and rhymes. From *Pat-a-Cake* to *Little Tommy Tucker,* from *Jack Sprat* to *Little Jack Horner,* food enters a child's education at the very early years. We sing about it, celebrate it, and suffer because we consume too much of it. It is only fitting therefore, that food also plays an important role in education through the integration of basic concepts in mathematics and science" (1987, iv).

Through the activities in *Incredible Edible Science*, children learn about food and cooking, and are introduced to concepts in science, mathematics, language, and literacy integrated with opportunities for social and emotional development. This aligns with one of the key messages of the National Association for the Education of Young Children (NAEYC) in *Developmentally Appropriate Practice in Early Childhood Programs*.

> All the domains of children's development and learning interrelate. For example, because social factors strongly influence cognitive development and academic competence—and the cognitive domain influences the social domain—teachers must foster learning and development in both, as well as in the emotional and physical domains. (Copple and Bredekamp 2009, xiii)

Incredible Edible Science activities are DAP (developmentally appropriate practice) in action, providing a hands-on tool for those of us seeking to provide strong child outcomes, achieve curriculum goals, and inspire children's curiosity and learning.

EARLY BRAIN DEVELOPMENT

Using the stimulating sensory, emotional, and socialization aspects of food experiences in the early childhood classroom enhances early brain development as it integrates the science process skills and language and literacy activities. Many research findings support our intuitive knowledge of how young children learn.

The first five to seven years of life are a sensitive period of rapid growth in brain development. Early brain research, or cognitive neuroscience research, provides us with information that can inform our knowledge of children and influence our teaching strategies. Some of the findings include the following:

- Brain development is a combination of both nature and experiences. "A stimulating environment—including reading, singing, talking and playing with a young child—is essential to brain development" (Landry 2005, 3).
- "Nurturing and stable relationships with caring adults are essential to healthy human development beginning from birth" (National Scientific Council on the Developing Child 2004, 2).
- "Young children learn through hands-on, activity-based sensory experiences. When their hands are active and they are learning through their senses, their brains are engaged" (Stephens 1999, 47).
- "The brain constantly tries to make sense of new information by making connections to previous experiences. Recognizing patterns and making connections out of those patterns and previous experiences help children make sense of the world" (Stephens 1999, 48).
- "Emotional engagement activates the brain. Both memory and motivation are impacted by these emotions" (Schiller 1999, 50).
- Although learning is a lifelong process, there are sensitive periods for acquiring different kinds of knowledge and skills. "Experiences during these sensitive periods play an exceptionally important role in shaping the capacities of the brain. Some examples of behavioral capacities that have been shown to be affected by sensitive periods of underlying circuitry include vision, hearing, language, and responses to social cues" (National Scientific Council on the Developing Child 2007, 2).

Specific cognitive processes that are important for teachers to understand about young children are those related to executive functioning, such as attention, memory, mental representation, logic and characteristics of thought, reasoning, concept acquisition, and classification. Using current brain research as a foundation for best practices means we have research-based knowledge, not just assumptions, to guide the decisions we make about an effective curriculum and teaching (Copple and Bredekamp 2009).

SCIENCE AND YOUNG CHILDREN

Science is naturally motivating to children. Young children have a sense of wonder, a natural desire to explore their world, and most are eager to create and discover. Children enter the world as natural investigators, are innately curious, and have a precious sense of wonder, asking questions such as "Why is the ocean blue?" "Why does it rain?" "Where does the water go after it rains?" "Where does a butterfly sleep?" "How does a worm see?" and "How does the electricity get into the wall?" For the young child, science is a search for this understanding. Young children use their senses as tools for scientific investigation, constantly probing, poking, tasting, and testing their surroundings, seeking to answer their own internal questions. Learning is often messy.

Incredible Edible Science encourages each child to be physically involved during the learning experience, which is an important brain-compatible strategy. The child's need to manipulate materials through free exploration is essential before a child can move on to more directive activities.

Kinesthetic sensing within the body and through the five senses helps the brain make those important critical connections. Kinesthetic sensing helps young children in learning how they are connected to the world and their relationship to their environment. Because of their investigative nature, brain-compatible hands-on science activities provide a great vehicle for children to learn as they explore.

In addition to engaging children's senses, this book's activities allow exploration, repetition, and extension to meet each child's unique needs and stage of development. These experiences allow children more time to see patterns and make connections, which is a foundation for later learning. One of the key messages of NAEYC's position statement on developmentally appropriate practice explains this:

> Developmentally appropriate practice does not mean making things easier for children. Rather, it means ensuring that goals and experiences are suited to their learning and development and challenging enough to promote their progress and interest. (Copple and Bredekamp 2009, xii)

THE SCIENCE, LANGUAGE, AND LITERACY CONNECTION

Language development is the process of learning to communicate ideas and express wants and needs. Learning to read and write are precursors to later school success. Participating in rich science experiences that engage the senses, integrate math, provide social contact, promote curiosity, and engage critical thinking skills is a strong motivator for making the language and literacy connection.

Incredible Edible Science supports developmentally appropriate experiences and teaching in literacy learning as recommended in the joint International Reading Association (IRA) and NAEYC position statement.

NAEYC and IRA recommend the following approaches:

> During the preschool years:
>
> - Positive, nurturing relationships with adults who engage in responsive conversations with individual children, model reading and writing behavior, and foster children's interest in and enjoyment of reading and writing;
> - Print-rich environments that provide opportunities and tools for children to see and use written language for a variety of purposes, with teachers drawing children's attention;
> - Opportunities for children to talk about what is read and to focus on the sounds and parts of language as well as the meaning;
> - Teaching strategies and experiences that develop phonemic awareness, such as songs, fingerplays, games, poems, and stories in which phonemic patterns such as rhyme and alliteration are salient;
> - Firsthand experiences that expand children's vocabulary, such as . . . exposure to various tools, objects, and materials.
>
> In kindergarten and primary grades:
>
> - Daily opportunities and teacher support to write many kinds of texts for different purposes, including stories, lists, messages to others, poems, reports, and responses to literature;
> - Writing experiences that allow the flexibility to use nonconventional forms of writing at first (invented or phonic spelling) and over time move to conventional forms;
> - Opportunities to work in small groups for focused instruction and collaboration with other children;
> - An intellectually engaging and challenging curriculum that expands knowledge of the world and vocabulary.
>
> (IRA and NAEYC 1998, 9–10)

Chapter 4, Blending Language and Literacy into Science Activities, provides a more thorough explanation of the integrated format connecting the activities with the position statement strategies.

SOCIAL-EMOTIONAL DEVELOPMENT AND YOUNG CHILDREN

Nurturing adults play an essential role in creating the critically important community for learning. "Early, secure attachments contribute to the growth of a broad range of competencies, including a love of learning, a comfortable sense of oneself, positive social skills, multiple successful relationships at later ages, and a sophisticated understanding of emotions, commitment, morality, and other aspects of human relationships" (National Scientific Council on the Developing Child 2004, 2). "When children, and not teaching children, are the focus, meaningful learning takes place" (Schickedanz 1986, 125).

Incredible Edible Science encourages teachers and children to work together in small groups. This provides greater opportunity for intimate communication and relationship development.

According to Copple and Bredekamp (2009), these are some of the many important aspects of social-emotional development in young children that teachers need to know about and that can be enhanced by working with children both individually and in small groups:

- social interactions, relationships with teachers and peers, and friendships
- development of prosocial behavior
- aggression and other challenging behaviors
- sense of self in relation to others
- development of emotional competence
- stress, coping, and resilience
- self-regulation

(Tomlinson and Hyson 2009, 111)

Teachers are constantly modeling how to behave with others. Their goal is to model what children need to learn. The young child's positive sense of self, ability to control emotions, and ability to negotiate with others are still evolving. Some children alienate other children by repeatedly making the same social mistakes, such as bullying or crying to get their way. Small-group experiences allow "scaffolding," a teaching approach that involves building upon what the child already knows by introducing new challenges one step at a time. Scaffolding assists the child in the self-management skills of negotiating, waiting, and listening respectfully to others.

Teachers need to have a relationship with each child and must be prepared to help each child develop the skills necessary to form relationships. No child should leave an early childhood classroom without making friends. Young children are often very egocentric in their thinking patterns, and social interactions help children to move out of this characteristic way of thinking. At the same time, they are social beings constantly interacting with others as they explore their world. An integrated curriculum with a strong science focus can be a vehicle for developing children's social skills and increasing their emotional intelligence. Warm relationships with families and teachers, and ample opportunities to socialize with other children are brain-compatible strategies for learning.

Social skills are a vital part of life. *Incredible Edible Science* activities encourage children to work with others, to exchange ideas and investigate different ways of thinking, and to experiment. It is part of the child's role as a scientific learner to collaborate and work cooperatively with peers.

Setting the Table for Learning

Cooking and food-related activities often require different forethought and preparation than other types of activities in which you engage the children. To help you "set the table for learning," here are some recommendations about communication, safety and health, materials and equipment, snack centers, and the role of the teacher in managing the activities and engaging in best practices to ensure your *Incredible Edible Science* activities progress smoothly.

STARTING OUT STRONG: COMMUNICATING WITH OTHERS

Communication is clearly one of the most important factors in almost any program or curriculum. Keeping others informed in advance can prevent many types of problems. Communicate often with everyone involved in your program.

Families

- Have families complete a form identifying any food allergies and the extent of the allergy, as well as the safety precautions required to protect the child. Check with a physician if the situation warrants.
- Keep an updated list of children and food allergies posted on your bulletin board. Refer to the list before each activity.
- Provide alternative snacks for children with food allergies.
- Keep families informed about activities and themes. Send home a wish list for materials and invite families to participate.

School

- Follow the policy at your center or school regarding food in the classroom.
- Have a plan for cleanup and disposal of left-over materials.
- If you have a cafeteria or kitchen staff, enlist their help. You may need to use their utensils or equipment.
- Share your plans with your peers and administration.

COOKING SAFETY AND HEALTH

Keeping the children in your care safe is of utmost importance. The immune systems of preschoolers are still developing, which can make them more prone to becoming ill. The USDA provides recommended food-safety guidelines online at www.choosemyplate.gov/preschoolers.

General Safety

- Be sure you review the posted list of children with allergies and choose appropriate products or alternatives for all activities.
- Be sure to follow standard food-safety practices in preparation, storage, and cooking, such as washing produce to remove any dirt, pesticides, or toxins, and refrigerating perishable items promptly.
- Equipment needs to be in excellent condition. Be sure there are no sharp edges, frayed plugs, or other hazards.
- Minimize the use of heat with young children. However, if a recipe calls for heat, use electric skillets or electric burners and appropriate cooking containers. The temperature is easier to control and the equipment can be removed for easy cleanup.

Location

- Be sure the activity location provides for safety relating to electrical outlets, has access to water for cleanup, and is away from the classroom traffic flow to minimize interruptions.
- If there is no direct access to water for cleanup, consider mixing materials in plastic bags by "squishing" and using reusable plastic tablecloths and/or inexpensive and disposable products such as newspapers.

Hand Washing and Surface Sanitation

- Always model and require appropriate hand-washing techniques as part of the process.
- For sanitary reasons, do not use the same equipment or utensils for both edible and inedible items. Use separate utensils for meats and other foods to avoid cross-contamination.
- Provide each child with his or her own materials and tools (mixing bowl, spoon, plastic knife, plate, and so on) to maximize sanitation.
- Clean all surfaces before and after an activity.

Choking Hazards

- Be sure to cut up food into pieces no larger than one-half inch and tell the children to chew their food well.
- Be sure the activities are age-appropriate and don't include foods or materials that might be hazardous to young children, since they sometimes attempt to swallow items whole. Here are some foods to avoid:
  - peanuts
  - popcorn
  - whole grapes
  - tough meat
  - chewing gum
  - cherry tomatoes
  - chips
  - hard candy
  - round slices of hot dogs or sausages
  - carrot sticks or baby carrots
  - large pieces of raw fruits and vegetables

MATERIALS AND EQUIPMENT

Cooking is easier when you have the materials and equipment you need. Set up one large plastic storage container with enough cooking utensils and implements to accommodate several groups of children. This will allow you to complete your activities with most of the class without interrupting the process to wash and sanitize. Wash, sanitize, and store materials and equipment when activities are complete. Whenever possible, "be green" by recycling and reusing materials instead of using paper products.

It is important for each child to have a hands-on experience with the cooking activities and not just sit and observe. Most activities can be done in small groups of four to five children, for example, during learning center time or outdoor time. We recommend the following materials to support multiple groups:

Measuring Tools

- eight one-cup plastic liquid measuring cups with handles
- two two-cup plastic liquid measuring cups with handles
- four sets of dry nesting measuring cups
- four sets of plastic metric measuring spoons
- plastic spoons, about the size of one tablespoon
- balancing scale
- food scale
- timer, stopwatch, minute glass, or egg timer

Containers

- twenty small plastic bowls such as whipped-topping tubs or butter tubs
- twenty small plastic plates
- small plastic or paper cups (see Nonperishable Consumables, next column)
- assorted metal or plastic containers
- four to eight large bowls
- assorted washable storage containers with lids

Tools

- two handheld egg beaters
- four small whisks
- tongs
- two wooden spoons
- five potato peelers (different kinds are fun for children)
- two apple corers and slicers
- two graters, one box-shaped grater and one flat grater
- one apple corer and peeler that cores and peels apples at the same time
- two rubber spatulas
- ten eyedroppers
- two kitchen basters
- two ear syringes
- four small magnifying glasses
- six dish towels
- two sponges
- spray bottle for sanitation

Nonperishable Consumables

- one box straws
- one hundred plastic spoons
- one hundred tongue depressors
- one hundred plastic knives
- aluminum foil
- waxed paper
- assorted zippered, resealable plastic storage bags
- paper bowls
- five-ounce paper cups
- paper plates
- paper towels or napkins

SNACK CENTERS

Children are more likely to taste something they make. As an alternative to group snacktime, which often involves a wait time for children, consider setting up a simple snack center where children can make their own snacks or engage in the science activity during learning-center time.

Introduce the snack center during large-group time as a new center. Provide a checklist so children can mark off their names. Monitor to encourage participation. Carefully review the procedure with the children, showing them a rebus recipe and/or demonstrating the activity. Cleanup and trash pickup is part of this process. You may want to include cleanup as part of the rebus recipe. Remind children of the importance of washing hands (be sure to monitor this with your "third eye").

Set up the snack center for two to four children, depending on your space, the children's ages, and the amount of supervision you are able to provide. With three- and four-year-olds, keep the snack construction simple. Here are some easy snack ideas:

- crackers with butter, cream cheese, or peanut butter
- fruit prepared in advance and available in individual servings
- half banana, peeled, cut in rounds, skewered on toothpicks, dipped in honey then in wheat germ

For five- to six-year-olds, snack activities may become more complex, with construction or mixing of ingredients. Again, a clear demonstration is important. With clear guidelines, children will soon begin to work independently.

THE ROLE OF THE TEACHER

> A teacher's moment-by-moment actions and interactions with children are the most powerful determinant of learning outcomes and development. Curriculum is very important, but what the teacher does is paramount. (Copple and Bredekamp 2009, xiii)

Managing the Activities

- Determine the group size and members in advance, based on the activity requirements, group dynamics, and individual needs. Consider individual interactions and classroom management issues as you select the activities.
- Review the activity in advance, particularly "Questions You Can Ask," so that you can be purposeful and intentional, flexible and open-ended. Add additional questions as needed to enrich the activity.
- Organize and prepare all materials in advance, including literacy and language materials, charts, books, and so on.
- Individualize instruction and be sensitive and flexible to children's needs and interests. Modify the activities by simplifying or adding additional steps to make the activities appropriate. Create a plan in advance for children who may finish quickly or work slowly.
- Consider involving older or more mature children as helpers.
- Establish a signal to give permission to eat.
- Plan your demonstration process and practice it in advance.
- Do activities in segments as appropriate. An example might be to read the related book and engage in the Sound Play activities during other segments of the day.
- Demonstrate and monitor safety and sanitation procedures during preparation and cleanup.

Best Practices

- Focus on the process instead of the outcome by creating a safe learning environment where children can explore and make mistakes.
- Set behavioral boundaries so children will feel safe and secure and understand appropriate boundaries for their behavior.
- Look for "teachable moments" and opportunities to scaffold and extend learning. Help children make connections and see relationships between what they are doing and math or literacy.
- Create a child-centered classroom that encourages active listening and joint excitement in learning. Be supportive and coach and encourage children in their learning.
- Be a scientific investigator. Model the science process and share your thinking and problem-solving ideas with the children.
- Provide periods of uninterrupted time for children to investigate materials and process activities and for incidental learning. Children's interest will dictate the time.

Cooking Up Basic Science Process Skills

One of the primary responsibilities in teaching young children science is to help them acquire the skills necessary to investigate and gather information about the world. These skills are often referred to by educators as "science process skills." Process skills have been described as the tools of scientific investigation. They are the tools and skills that scientists use as they conduct their investigations. Similarly, even for young children, these skills are the tools they can use as they begin to explore their personal world. Toddlers are keen observers as they examine the environment around themselves and begin to sort objects according to size, color, and shape. The young child pouring rice, sand, or water into containers of different sizes or building blocks into tall structures and seeing them tumble down again and again is beginning to use these skills.

SIX BASIC SCIENCE PROCESS SKILLS

For young children, the basic science process skills are the most important for them to acquire:

- observing
- classifying
- communicating
- measuring
- inferring
- predicting

Even though young children are often able to perceive their natural surroundings and are born with a powerful desire to do so, specific science process skills still need to be taught. In fact, all teachers have a basic responsibility of planning short and simple science activities that are designed to help children acquire, practice, and refine these science process skills. These activities may suggest science concepts yet are specifically designed for giving children practice with the skills.

The following sections describe each of the process skills appropriate for young children and provide some suggested activities for developing the skill.

Observing

Observing is one of the most basic skills young children can develop. A good observer is able to see, hear, smell, taste, and feel objects with great skill. Making connections through the senses and problem solving are brain-compatible learning strategies that increase the number of neural pathways in the brain. Children, who develop these five senses and thus their skill of observing, relate to the world around them with greater accuracy and greater depth. Observation skills, particularly phonological awareness (listening), are essential tools in becoming a better reader and possibly a more successful learner in many other areas.

Making observations is one of the scientist's most fundamental skills. Similarly, as scientists conduct their investigations, they must use their five senses to obtain information regarding their experiments. We use our senses every day to acquire information about the world. With young children, observation usually focuses on properties of objects (color, size, shape, and so on) and patterns in the environment. It is important to remember that young children need to move slowly through the observation process in the beginning. They need a guided tour to assist them in focusing on the small details and appreciating the fine nuances occurring in using the five senses. Furthermore, this depth of observation also lends itself to rich opportunities in language development.

For young children, the science cooking/food activities in this chapter are helpful in developing the skill of making observations. Because observation can be defined as learning about one's world through the five senses, these observation activities are separated, with related cooking/food activities provided for each sense: sight, smell, taste, touch, and sound.

Sight Children use their eyes to observe similarities and/or differences between objects and events. Our sense of sight enables us to know the size and shape of objects. "Eighty percent of the information received by the brain comes in through our eyes" (Gossett, Delano, Kramer, Welk, and Wood 1994, 2).

Smell Children use their noses to determine if things have an odor or not. They also use their noses to determine the many different scents of objects and the strengths of those scents.

Taste Children use their tongues to determine how something tastes. The human tongue has taste receptor cells that help identify four main taste sensations: salty, sour, sweet, bitter. Combined with the sense of smell, these four taste sensations give humans the sensation of flavor.

Touch Children can use their hands and feet to determine many characteristics of different materials and objects using the sense of touch. Children also use their mouths to observe the texture of food by comparing cooked and uncooked vegetables. This helps them to understand that their mouth can work much like their hands as a tool for observation.

Sound Children use their ears to determine characteristics of objects related to sound such as frequencies, pitch, tone, rhythm, and strength of a sound. Listening to, making, and sharing sounds with others are enjoyable activities for young children and provide a foundation for other simple science concepts.

Classifying

Classification is a skill used daily in the lives of both children and adults. Most children begin at a very early age naturally arranging various objects in their world into groups. They classify crayons, toys, books, clothes, kitchen utensils, and so on into different groups or sets. Very young children often classify such objects according to size, color, and shape. Older children can make more complex differentiations based on such attributes as number concepts, function, mass, volume, and so on. Adults also live in a world based on complex classification schemes. Cars, grocery items, clothes, and departments in stores and offices are all classified and arranged according to some grouping plan. Therefore, classification is a very natural and relevant skill.

Similarly, to investigate the world, scientists classify objects in their environment. Biologists, geologists, chemists, physicists, and environmentalists all use extensive classifications systems to organize their investigations and work. This process of classification consists of identifying an attribute that is common to certain elements of a collection and then grouping the elements accordingly. In addition, classification activities encourage the growth of clear, logical thinking, which is the basis of sound scientific reasoning. Classification activities serve as an excellent introduction to other science process skills, enabling all children to experience success in a fun and meaningful way.

Communicating

An important skill for children and adults is the ability to express themselves in oral or in written form. This skill, fundamental to all academic subjects, is basic to the sciences. A scientific discovery has little utility if it is not communicated to others in the field who can then use the findings or subject them to independent verification. For that reason, it is not surprising that communication is considered a fundamental process skill for scientists. Similarly, when children are provided with the opportunity to record and reflect upon an experience, the increased exposure enables them to strengthen their understanding of the concepts learned. This opportunity for individual reflection also gives the teacher an occasion for assessment as to understandings and misconceptions held by a child.

Scientists use several types of communication to share their investigative findings, including drawings, pictures, models, data/worksheets, lab reports, tables, charts, graphs, journals, and oral communication. Pictures can be an effective means for children to express themselves. This is especially true for younger children, who may not have other well-developed communication skills. Older children may also have difficulty putting thoughts into words, but may be capable of eloquently expressing their ideas through the use of pictures. For example, after children learn about how plants grow, a teacher could ask children to draw a series of pictures describing the different stages in a plant's growth. Or children may look at a piece of moldy bread using a magnifying lens and then draw a picture of what they see. After a field trip to a bakery, children could be asked to draw pictures of what they observed in the bakery.

Examples of other communication strategies used in early childhood classrooms include pictures, rebus recipes, models, charts, graphic organizers, nonverbal communication, oral communication, journals, labels, and narratives.

Measuring

Measurement is one of the most practical process skills in science because it is central to our everyday lives. Many of the fundamental concepts of measurement are so basic to us that we rarely think of them. When we make fundamental daily comparisons, however, we are using the skill of measurement, because making comparisons is the basis for measurement. Here are some examples:

- Jane stops pouring milk in her glass when her comparison of the amount of milk to the size of the glass tells her that the glass is in danger of overflowing.
- Juan rushes home when he notices it is growing dark outside and so it must be getting late.
- Anisa compares two dresses and decides that one fits better than the other.

Each of these comparisons is simple, general, and approximate in nature, yet is quite typical of basic comparative activities we are involved with daily. More specifically, the ability to use measuring tools and instruments is vital to our everyday lives in such areas as measuring of time in surveying, describing, and predicting weather; measuring environmental noise and air pollution; measuring human attitude and aptitude; and measuring automobile speed, gasoline volume, water level, oil pressure, and electrical charge.

These types of measurement demands for adults have resulted in increased concern for teaching our children measurement skills. Concepts and skills in the area of measurement all deal with the idea of making a comparison between what is being measured and some suitable standard of measure. The key to developing skills in measurement is to provide children with ample experiences through measurement activities. Put simply, children learn how to measure by measuring. The experience and excitement of measuring is a motivational factor in getting children to learn measurement concepts.

According to Burns, when organizing classroom measurement activities, four successive stages in learning need to be considered:

1. Making comparisons between objects by matching. Children compare objects by matching, without the use of other tools of measurement. They order things by this method of comparison.
2. Comparing objects with nonstandard units. Children use a variety of objects for measuring—parts of the body, straws, cubes, books, and whatever else is readily available.
3. Comparing objects with standard units. Standard units should emerge as a convenient extension of nonstandard units, useful for the purpose of communication. It makes sense that children become comfortable with both the metric and English systems. We live in a "bilingual" measurement world, and children need to be familiar with both ways of measuring.
4. Choosing suitable units for specific measurements. Children learn to select the appropriate standard units of measurement needed for specific applications.

(Burns 2007, 70–72)

It is difficult and usually not even possible to say precisely at what ages children can become competent in each of these four stages. However, a general guideline is that younger children should be involved with measurement activities using direct comparisons and nonstandard units to make comparisons. After these skills have been obtained, then children are ready for activities that emphasize making comparisons using selected standard units of measure and that help children to choose suitable units for specific measurement.

Inferring

Making inferences is a central part of a scientist's work. Being able to observe a situation, experiment, and then explain or describe why something happened the way it did is an important skill. Inferring is often described as explaining or interpreting an observation or sets of observations that have taken place in the past. They may include drawing conclusions, generalizing, analyzing, theorizing, evaluating, interpreting, and asking "Why did that happen" type questions. Inferences, then, are statements that attempt to show a relationship between two or more observations. Inferences are often confused with making observations. Observations are statements based on something one actually felt, heard, saw, smelled, or tasted, whereas inferences are explanations or interpretations of these observations. Children should learn to realize that the more observations they take into account, the more valid their inferences will be.

We have a better appreciation of our environment when we are able to interpret and explain things happening around us. We learn to recognize patterns and expect these patterns to reoccur under the same conditions. Much of our own behavior is based on the inferences we make about events. Scientists form hypotheses based on the inferences they make regarding their investigations. As teachers, we constantly make inferences about why our children behave as they do. Learning in itself is an inference made from observed changes in learner behavior.

Predicting

As one thinks about scientists performing investigations, one realizes the importance of their ability to predict certain events. Meteorologists, for example, use this skill as they predict movement of hurricanes, thunderstorms, and other weather patterns. Predicting is usually defined as making forecasts of future events based upon observations or inferences. Predicting the future involves using known data, logical reasoning, estimating, guessing, thinking ahead, and projecting.

Predictions are based on observations and inferences. Scientists, for example, will make a forecast into the future based on something they observed yesterday or even days and weeks ago. Similarly, they will make a prediction based on an inference they made as well. Therefore, predicting is closely related to other process skills such as classifying, inferring, and observing. Predicting is a great example of how one process skill can be dependent on other process skills. The skill of making predictions depends on the skill of making careful observations and inferences based on what has been observed.

For a summary showing the specific science process skill each activity in chapter 3 promotes, see the chart in appendix B.

OBSERVING/SIGHT

Look and See

Words You Can Use

potholder, rolling pin, spatula, utensils

What You Need

- three or four cooking utensils or items such as a rolling pin, can opener, spatula, potholder
- cloth for hiding utensils

What You Do

1. Gather the children in a circle.
2. Select three or more familiar utensils.
3. Place them in a pile or in a straight line.
4. Ask the children to look at the utensils very carefully as you identify them.
5. Cover the utensils.
6. Ask the children to close or cover their eyes.
7. Remove one of the items and hide it.
8. Ask the children to look and see.
9. Let the children guess which item or utensil is missing.
10. Add or remove more than one utensil or item as children become more observant.
11. Ask them to share how they remembered what was missing.

Questions You Can Ask

- *How many items did you see?*
- *Which one is missing?*

OBSERVING/SIGHT

Which Lemon Is Mine?

Words You Can Use

bumpy, dimpled, lemon, rough, smooth

What You Need

- one lemon for each child
- basket

What You Do

1. Arrange the children in small groups.
2. Give each child a lemon.
3. Help each child examine her lemon carefully for distinguishing features as later each child must be able to pick out her lemon from a mixed group of lemons.
4. Help the children with the vocabulary that could be used to describe their lemons (rough, smooth, dimpled, bumpy, and so on).
5. Tell the children that the lemons are their "babies" and that soon they will be leaving their lemon babies at school to play with other lemon babies. Their babies cannot talk yet, so it is very important that each child be able to identify her lemon baby.
6. Ask the children to put their lemons in the basket.
7. Mix up the lemons.
8. Have the children pick out their lemon babies and describe the distinguishing features, or attributes, that helped them identify their own lemon baby.

Note: Do not use the lemon babies to make lemonade. Some children may become very attached to their babies.

Questions You Can Ask

- *What does your lemon look like?*
- *How is your lemon special?*
- *What does your lemon feel like?*
- *How is your lemon different from other children's lemons?*
- *What are some things you like about your lemon?*

OBSERVING/SIGHT

Sha Zam! Food Changes Form!

Words You Can Use

curds, form, grate, mash, peel, processed, squeeze, whey

What You Need

- various foods and utensils, depending on which activity or activities you decide to do
- chart paper divided into "before" and "after" observation categories

What You Do

Let the children assist you in changing the form of the food so they can observe the difference between its original form and its processed form. Be sure to have children observe each food carefully. You can record their "before" and "after" observations on chart paper.

Gum

Have the children observe their pieces of gum before, during, and after chewing them.

Note: All Wrigley gum products have a W on the gum that can be used for letter recognition.

Carrots

Use carrots with stems. Wash, cut into strips or rounds, cut and cook, peel, grate, make salad, or have a peel-and-grate center.

Oranges

Peel and section, cut, squeeze, and pour into a glass. Use different kinds of oranges and orange-juice squeezers.

Potatoes

Wash and bake, peel, cut, cook, and mash or fry. Make mashed potato sculptures by forming shapes. Geometry terms such as "circle," "square," "cube," and "sphere" can be used.

Cream

Pour heavy whipping cream in a baby-food jar and place a marble in it. Screw the lid on tightly and shake to make butter. Spread on crackers.

Milk

Add different flavorings to milk, such as chocolate, strawberry, or maple syrup.

Milk (continued)

Make Miss Muffet's curds and whey. Warm two cups of milk, then add one teaspoon of vinegar. Curds (the milk solids) will separate from the whey (the liquid). Strain the curds from the whey by pouring through cheesecloth. Dump the curds onto a paper towel and gently press the curds with more towels to remove the liquid. Sprinkle with salt and refrigerate until ready to eat. The curds can be served at room temperature and eaten as a cottage cheese. Or stir them until they are smooth and add different flavorings, such as cinnamon, orange flavoring, or vanilla. Spread the curds on crackers. Curds also taste good with peanut butter.

Caution: Take all necessary safety precautions with cooking and utensils such as graters (see chapter 2).

Questions You Can Ask

- *What were some of the foods you used today?*
- *How did they look before they were changed? After they were changed?*
- *What were some ideas we shared and wrote on our before-and-after chart?*

OBSERVING/SIGHT

Flavored Gelatin: Sink or Float?

Words You Can Use

float, grated, sink, sliced

What You Need

- flavored gelatin
- blueberries
- sliced bananas
- sliced peaches
- strawberries
- grated coconut
- index cards to label fruits
- water
- large mixing spoon
- bowls or containers (one for each flavor of gelatin)
- chart paper or drawing paper for each child
- crayons

What You Do

1. Let children help you mix several containers of flavored gelatin. Follow the directions on the package.
2. Show the children the assortment of fruits you plan to put into the gelatin. Help them name each fruit and match it to its label.

Note: Do not use pineapple, as gelatin does not congeal when mixed with this fruit.

3. Let the children tell you which ones they think will sink and which ones they think will float when the gelatin is ready. Record their guesses on a chart with columns labeled "sink" or "float," or let each child draw her own chart with "sink" and "float" columns.
4. Add a variety of fruits to the containers of gelatin and refrigerate until gelatin is set. (This may take several hours or overnight.)
5. Assist children in examining the gelatin to see which objects sank or floated.
6. Have children compare their original observations to the results. Have them draw the results on their papers or record them on the class chart.

Note: You can tape the index cards to the chart paper instead of rewriting the fruit names.

Questions You Can Ask

- *Which fruits floated in the gelatin?*
- *Which fruits sank in the gelatin?*

OBSERVING/SIGHT

Can You Guess the Color?

Words You Can Use

black, blue, brown, green, orange, purple, red, yellow

What You Need

- fruits and/or vegetables in a variety of colors, such as brown, blue, green, orange, purple, red, and yellow (be sure to include an apple, a banana, and an orange)
- tray for each small group of children
- brown lunch bag for each small group of children

What You Do

1. Prepare mixed bags of fruits and/or vegetables ahead of time by putting an assortment into brown lunch bags.
2. Separate children into small groups.
3. Give each group a bag of fruits and/or vegetables.
4. Have the children open the bags and place the food items on the tray.
5. Suggest that the items on the tray are alike in a couple of ways.
6. Ask the children how the items are alike. Allow time for them to answer.
7. Ask the children to arrange their fruits and vegetables in ways that show how they are alike.
8. If color is not suggested as a way of arranging the fruits and vegetables, then tell the children that one way the items are alike is that some of them are the same color.
9. Hold up several pieces of fruits and vegetables of a specific color as an example.
10. Model for the children how to rearrange, or sort, the items on the tray by color.
11. Then ask the children to find something on their tray that is also that color.
12. Proceed through the other colors in the same way.
13. For assessment, bring in other food items of the same color, such as other fruits and vegetables, pieces of candy, or a variety of peppers.
14. Hold each of the items up and have the children tell its color.

Questions You Can Ask

- *How did we sort the fruits and vegetables?*
- *What is the color of the banana? The apple? The orange?*

OBSERVING/SIGHT

Pea Puddles

Words You Can Use

absorb, peas, soak

What You Need

- black-eyed peas or similar peas
- plastic container
- plate or tray slightly bigger than the plastic container
- water
- a piece of paper for each child, divided in half and labeled "before" and "after"
- crayons

What You Do

1. Early in the day, fill the plastic container with peas and place it on a tray.
2. Add water. There should be enough water and peas so the peas are about level with the plastic container's top edge.
3. Gather the children around the container filled with peas.
4. Have the children make all the observations they can and draw a picture of what they see on the "before" side of their papers.
5. Set the peas and container aside for several hours.
6. After a few hours, have the children observe the peas and container again. Let them share their observations with the group.
7. Discuss their observations. (The peas will become large by absorbing the water and will spill over onto the tray.)
8. Now have the children draw what they observe on the "after" side of their papers.

Questions You Can Ask

- *How have the peas changed from when they were first put in the container?*
- *What do you think happened to the peas after they sat in the water for a while?*

OBSERVING/SIGHT

Coconut Crazy

Words You Can Use

brown, coconut, hairy, milky, sweet

What You Need

- one coconut for each small group of children
- one magnifying glass for each small group of children
- screwdriver to puncture coconuts
- hammer to crack open coconuts
- plastic tray for each small group of children
- cups
- pitcher
- towel to cover the coconut while breaking
- chart paper for recording observations or drawing paper for each child
- crayons

What You Do

1. Separate the children into small groups.
2. Give each group a coconut.
3. Have them observe the coconut using a magnifying glass.
4. Help them make all the observations they can about the coconut.
5. Listen to their observations and record them on chart paper.
6. Create a nest with the towel to support the coconut while you punch out the eyes using the screwdriver. (The eyes are the softer, darker part of the coconut.) Place the screwdriver over one eye at a time and hammer on the eye until you break through the coconut shell.
7. Drain the coconut milk into a pitcher. Then pour small servings into cups for each child to taste.
8. Have the children describe how the milk tastes. Write their descriptions on the chart paper.
9. Wrap the coconut completely in the towel and hammer on it with the hammer until it cracks open. Try hitting around the equator of the coconut for ease in breaking. The towel will prevent the shell pieces from flying everywhere.
10. Have the children once again make all the observations they can about the coconut now that it is cracked.
11. Record their observations on chart paper or let them draw their observations on paper.

Questions You Can Ask

- *How does the coconut look on the outside? On the inside?*
- *What does it feel like on the outside? On the inside?*
- *What does the coconut milk taste like?*
- *What does the coconut milk smell like?*
- *What does the coconut milk look like? How does the coconut milk look different from the milk you drink?*

OBSERVING/SIGHT

Sugar Rainbow

Words You Can Use

blue, crystals, disappear, green, mixture, red, stir, sugar, yellow

What You Need

- two teaspoons of sugar
- ten teaspoons of water
- aluminum-foil dishes, such as pie tins
- food coloring (blue, green, red, yellow)
- spoons
- bowl
- one piece of manila paper to make a class rainbow
- school glue

What You Do

1. Gather the children around.
2. Spoon the water into the bowl. Encourage the children to help you count the ten teaspoons of water as you put them in the bowl.
3. Let the children count as you add the sugar to the water. Stir the sugar and water mixture until the sugar disappears.
4. Pour two teaspoons of this mixture into each foil dish.
5. Add a different color of food coloring to each of the dishes, stirring gently to mix.
6. Place the dishes in a warm place for approximately three days.
7. After three days, have the children observe what happened. The water will evaporate after about three days and what's left behind will be colored sugared crystals.
8. Have the children break the crystals apart using a spoon.
9. The crystals from several pans can be arranged and glued on paper to make a class "sugar rainbow."

Questions You Can Ask

- *What happened to the sugar when it was stirred into water?*
- *What did the sugar and water grow?*
- *What do you think* evaporate *means?*

OBSERVING/SIGHT

Baggie Bread

Words You Can Use

dry, mold, sprinkle, warm, wet

What You Need

- two slices of white bread
- two resealable plastic sandwich baggies
- small tray
- water
- tape
- permanent marker
- chart paper or drawing paper for each child
- crayons

What You Do

1. Gather the children in a group.
2. Put one slice of bread in a plastic bag.
3. Pass around the other slice of bread. Ask the children to make observations about how the bread feels. Record their observations on chart paper or let children draw their observations on paper.
4. Place this slice of bread on a tray in a warm sunny place.
5. Let the bread sit there until it feels very dry. This may take several hours or overnight.
6. Show children the dried-out bread and record their observations of how the bread feels now that it is dried out.
7. Next, remove the other slice of bread from the plastic bag and sprinkle a few drops of water on it.
8. Put each slice of bread in a plastic baggie and seal the bags. (Leave some air in each bag.)
9. With a permanent marker, label the bag with dry bread in it "dry" and label the other bag "wet."
10. Place both bags on a tray in a warm place.
11. After three or four days, have the children observe the bags of bread again. Record their observations. (Since mold grows on wet food, the children should see mold on the bread in the bag labeled "wet.")
12. Discard the bags of bread after the experiment.

Questions You Can Ask

- *What did the fresh piece of bread feel like?*
- *What did the dry piece of bread feel like?*
- *What did the wet bread look like after three or four days?*
- *What did the dry bread look like after three or four days?*

OBSERVING/SIGHT

Pretty Penny

Words You Can Use

acid, cola, copper, dull, shiny

What You Need

- two dirty copper pennies
- two clear plastic cups
- cola
- chart paper or drawing paper for each child
- crayons

What You Do

1. Gather the children in a circle.
2. Place a dirty copper penny in each plastic cup.
3. Let the children make observations of the pennies in the cups. Record their observations on chart paper.
4. Let the children watch you open a cola. Ask them what they know about this drink product.
5. Pour the cola over one penny. Put both plastic cups side by side.
6. Have the children make observations of the pennies. Record their observations or have them draw what they see on paper.
7. Ask the children, "What do you think might happen to the pennies after a few days?"
8. Leave one penny in the cola for a few days. Leave the other penny in its empty cup.
9. Gather the children again and let them observe while you pour the cola off the penny. Discard the cola.
10. Have the children observe both pennies again. Discuss and record their observations. (The acid in the cola should have been strong enough to clean the penny and make it shine, while the other penny will still be dull.)

Questions You Can Ask

- *What did the penny look like before it was covered in cola?*
- *What did it look like after being in the cola for a while?*
- *What do you think happened to the penny in the cola?*

OBSERVING/SIGHT

Egg-Carton Rainbows

Words You Can Use

blue, compartments, egg carton, eyedropper, food coloring, red, yellow

What You Need

- one white foam egg carton (with top removed) for each child
- one eyedropper for each child
- water (bottled or in pitchers)
- food coloring in blue, red, and yellow
- one apron or old shirt for each child

What You Do

1. Have each child put on an apron or old shirt.
2. Place the egg cartons at a table and fill each compartment of the egg cartons about half full of water.
3. Have each child sit with an egg carton in front of him.
4. In each child's egg carton, add a drop of each food coloring to three of the egg compartments—one color per compartment. (This will leave nine compartments uncolored.)
5. Give each child an eyedropper and have him create other colors by mixing the colors in different compartments.
6. Give the children just a few minutes to freely explore making new colors.
7. Have the children discuss their findings.

Questions You Can Ask

- *What happened to the water when you added food coloring?*
- *What happened to the water when you mixed the colors together?*
- *What is your favorite color?*
- *What new colors did you make?*
- *How did you make a new color?*

OBSERVING/SIGHT

Cucumber Magic

Words You Can Use

absorb, cucumber, soak, sprinkle, water droplets

What You Need

- two or three cucumbers
- plastic spoon
- one teaspoon of sugar for each small group of children
- plates
- knife
- chart paper
- drawing paper
- crayons

What You Do

1. Prepare ahead by slicing the cucumbers into rounds. Place half of the sliced cucumbers on one plate and half on another plate.
2. Gather the children together.
3. Ask them to closely observe and touch the cucumbers on both plates. Guide them to note what the cucumbers look like and feel like. Record their responses on chart paper.
4. Select one child to sprinkle a small amount of sugar on one plate of cucumbers.
5. Let this plate of cucumbers sit for about ten minutes. (The sugar will draw the water from the cucumber. As the sugar absorbs the water, droplets will form on the surface of the cucumber slices.)
6. Have the children observe both plates of cucumber slices again.
7. Ask them what they observe. They should see that the cucumber slices sprinkled with sugar have big water droplets on them now, and that the cucumber slices without sugar do not have water droplets on them. Sugar absorbed the water so well that it drew the water from the cucumber.
8. Discuss the children's observations.
9. Allow the children to draw "before" and "after" pictures of the cucumber slices.

Questions You Can Ask

- *What did the cucumber slices look like at first?*
- *How did they look after they were sprinkled with sugar?*
- *What did you see forming on the cucumber slices?*

OBSERVING/SMELL

Can You Guess the Odor?

Words You Can Use

chopped, chunks, crushed, mint, pat, sharp, spicy, sour, sweet, tangy

What You Need

- eight baby-food jars
- small pats of mustard
- chopped onions
- crushed pieces of peppermint
- chopped pickles
- crushed cinnamon candy
- small chunks of cheese
- small pats of catsup
- small drop of syrup
- index cards with labeled pictures of the food items (cut pictures from grocery-store flyers or print them from a copyright-free Web site)
- blindfold made from a folded bandana or scarf
- whole coffee beans
- chart paper

What You Do

1. Prepare ahead by placing each of the edible items listed above into separate baby-food jars. Attach the lid to each jar to contain the smell.
2. Gather the children together.

3. Have one child guess the contents of the eight jars by smelling them.

Note: After the child smells two jars, have her smell the coffee beans to neutralize the previous odors.

4. Repeat this activity until all the children have had a turn smelling the contents of the jars.
5. Allow the children to guess what they might be smelling. Assist the children in practicing the names of the items in the jars, referring to the index cards when necessary. Discuss the children's responses and record them on chart paper.
6. After all of the children have smelled and guessed the contents of all the jars, blindfold one child.
7. Choose any jar and let the child guess its contents while blindfolded.

more →

8. Continue choosing jars for the child to smell and guess the contents of until the child has smelled all of the remaining seven jars.
9. Allow the child to describe how smelling the jars while blindfolded was different from smelling them without the blindfold.
10. After doing this activity once with the children, prepare jars with different contents and repeat on a different day.

Questions You Can Ask

- *What did you smell in the first jar?*
- *Do you think the smells were hard to guess? If yes, why and which ones?*
- *What was your favorite smell?*
- *What was the smell you liked the least?*

OBSERVING/SMELL

Can You Know without the Nose?

Words You Can Use

aroma, bitter, clogged, toasted, salty, slice, soft, sour, sweet

What You Need

- toast
- lemon
- nuts
- pretzels
- garlic
- index cards with labeled pictures of the food items (cut pictures from grocery-store flyers or print them from a copyright-free Web site)
- paper napkins
- plates

What You Do

1. Prepare ahead by toasting a piece of bread and slicing a lemon into quarters.
2. Put each of the items listed on a separate plate.
3. Cover each plate with a napkin.
4. Gather the children together.
5. Invite the children to smell the covered plates one plate at a time. After smelling one plate, let them discuss what they smell by asking, "Can you guess what it is if you cannot see or taste it?"
6. Follow this same procedure for each of the food items listed.
7. Next, have the children hold their noses and determine whether they can smell one of the items or another one. Let them try. Discuss the results.

Note: Some children may have difficulty holding their noses, so you or another adult may have to gently hold their noses for them.

8. Discuss how important our noses are for helping us smell different things correctly.
9. Uncover the plates and show them the items. Share the index card labels at this time.
10. Allow the children to smell the items again, and discuss their responses.
11. Ask the children if they have ever had difficulty smelling or tasting things when their nose was clogged due to a cold.
12. Discuss and share the children's observations, using words from the index cards to help reinforce vocabulary.

Questions You Can Ask

- *Why is smelling important and which body part helps us smell things?*
- *Which smell was your favorite?*
- *Which one(s) did you not like very well?*
- *What differences did you notice when you smelled the items covered and uncovered?*

OBSERVING/SMELL

Matching Odors

Words You Can Use

bay oil, cilantro, cinnamon, cotton ball, flavor, lemon, mint, opaque, strawberry, vanilla

What You Need

- opaque containers such as margarine tubs or film canisters
- cotton balls
- flavor extracts such as lemon, vanilla, strawberry, bay oil, cinnamon, cilantro, or mint
- index cards labeled with the scent or flavor names and showing related pictures (cut pictures from grocery-store flyers or print them from a copyright-free Web site)
- coffee beans

What You Do

1. Prepare ahead by making matching sets of scented cotton balls. Place a few drops of the same extract on two separate cotton balls. Repeat with each extract you have, to form two full sets.
2. Put one cotton ball in each of the plastic containers to create matching scents, for example, two containers with vanilla scents and two with almond scents.
3. Put the lids on only one set of containers. Leave the lids off the second set; place the lids under the containers.
4. Now gather the children.
5. Practice saying the words for the different scents and flavors, using the index cards as a guide.
6. Now have the children take turns smelling one uncovered container. Have them say what they think the scent is.
7. Then have the children try to pick the matching scent from the covered containers by smelling the different containers after removing the lids. Children may need to smell a few coffee beans in between sniffs as coffee beans will neutralize the odors of previous scents.
8. When the children find matching scents, have them line up the containers that they think match and identify the smell. If they need help, they can use the scent index cards. Check for accuracy.
9. Discuss with the children which odors were difficult to match as well as other observations about the activity. Try to use the words from the scent index cards.
10. These containers can be put in a science center after the activity.

Questions You Can Ask

- *Which smells were you able to match?*
- *Which smells were you not able to match?*

OBSERVING/SMELL

Does It Smell or Not?

Words You Can Use

shoe box, wrapper

What You Need

- shoe boxes
- a variety of food products that have scents, such as oranges, lemons, bananas, onions
- various food items that are unscented or cannot be smelled because they are in wrappers, such as packaged fruit roll-ups, canned vegetables or fruits, or canned orange juice
- index cards with labeled pictures of the food items (cut pictures from grocery-store flyers or print them from a copyright-free Web site)

What You Do

1. Prepare ahead by labeling one shoe box "smell" and the other shoe box "no smell."
2. Gather the children together.
3. Identify the items to be smelled and practice saying their names using the pictures on the index cards and the real items.
4. Discuss the meaning of the word "scent."
5. Model for the children how to carefully smell an object and decide whether to put it in the "smell" or "no smell" box.
6. Have the children take turns smelling the objects and placing them in the correct boxes.
7. Discuss the activity with the children. Try to use the words from the scent index cards.

Questions You Can Ask

- *What were some of the things that had no smell?*
- *What were some of the things that did have a smell?*
- *Were there any smells you liked or did not like? Which ones?*

OBSERVING/SMELL

Sniff Identification

Words You Can Use

gauze, scent

What You Need

- small plastic containers about the size of baby-food jars
- gauze
- strong-smelling food items such as peppercorns, cinnamon sticks, cloves, onion flakes, lemon pepper, peanuts, cocoa, or tea
- coffee beans
- picture cards that match the scents
- construction paper
- glue
- scissors
- chart paper

What You Do

1. Prepare ahead by wrapping the items with distinct smells in gauze.
2. Seal each wrapped item in a plastic container.
3. Make scent picture cards that match the scents of the foods you have chosen. You can cut out pictures from grocery-store flyers or print from a copyright-free Web site.
4. Glue the pictures to construction paper and trim the cards.
5. Gather the children.
6. Place the sealed containers before the group.
7. Spread out the scent picture cards so all the children can see them. Be sure the children know the words that go with each picture.
8. Assist the children in opening one container at a time. Pass the container around.
9. Then have the children take turns choosing the picture card that matches what they think they smelled in the container.
10. Place the picture card the children chose next to the container.
11. Pass around another scent and have the children repeat the process of choosing its matching picture card.
12. After the children have smelled two different scents, pass around an open container of coffee beans. This will neutralize the previous scents so the process of smelling more scents can continue to be effective.
13. Repeat the process until all scents have been matched to picture cards.
14. Allow children to rearrange their matching cards as they gain more information about the scents.
15. Discuss the results and write the words used for the different scents on chart paper.

Questions You Can Ask

- *Of all the containers, which scent do you like the best?*
- *Which one is your least favorite?*
- *Which scent smells the strongest?*

OBSERVING/SMELL

Shoe Box of Scents

Words You Can Use

smelly, strongest

What You Need

- shoe box
- scissors
- tape
- items with strong scents such as a lemon or cinnamon stick
- index cards with labeled pictures of the scented items (cut pictures from grocery-store flyers or print them from a copyright-free Web site)
- gauze

What You Do

1. Prepare ahead by cutting a hole in the middle of each side (not end) of the shoe box.
2. Using a marker, number the holes 1 and 2. The holes should be large enough for a child's nose to fit through to smell an item.
3. Wrap a scented item in gauze to conceal it.
4. Use tape to secure the gauze-wrapped item to the inside of the box near one hole. The item should be closer to one hole than the other so the children can smell the difference in intensity of the item.
5. Gather the children into small groups of two or three.
6. Pass the shoe box to one child at a time.
7. With his eyes closed, have the child smell into each hole until he guesses what the item is and can express which hole gives off the strongest smell.
8. Pass the shoe box to the next child, and see if the results are the same.
9. Lead the children to discuss their experiences and findings using the words on the scent cards. Have the scent cards nearby for the children's reference.

Questions You Can Ask

- *Did you guess what the scented item was?*
- *What was it?*
- *How did it smell?*
- *Which hole gave off the strongest smell? Why do you think that might be so?*

OBSERVING/SMELL

Sniff Walk

Words You Can Use

incense

What You Need

- one long table
- long, thin piece of cloth to cover the objects on the table
- three of each of the following: lemons, oranges, soap, bell peppers, onions
- pieces of cloth or cotton balls with extract scents on them such as vanilla, coffee, flowers, grapefruit, tangerine, incense, and essential oils
- one sticker for each sniffing station and extras for keeping score
- index cards with labeled pictures of the scented items (cut pictures from grocery-store flyers or print them from a copyright-free Web site)
- drawing paper labeled "I think I will smell this" on one side and "I know I smelled this" on the other side
- drawing paper
- crayons

What You Do

1. Prepare a smelling table in advance by placing objects on one side of the table, putting similar objects together.
2. Cover the objects lightly with a long, thin piece of cloth so children cannot see the objects.
3. Place a sticker to mark each sniffing station.
4. Guide one child at a time from one end of the table to the other, smelling each object through the cloth along the way.
5. As soon as the child smells a different odor, have the child say, "Change!"
6. Continue down the table reporting odor changes.
7. As children detect a small change in odors, place a sticker on their shirts. Children can compare how many stickers they each earned as a way to keep score.
8. As children wait for their turn, they can draw what they think they will smell on one side of their drawing paper, and when they complete their sniff walk, they can draw what they know they smelled on the other side.
9. Lead the children in discussing their findings after everyone has had a turn. Refer to the index cards to review the names of the scents.

Questions You Can Ask

- *What objects did you smell?*
- *Which objects did you think smelled the best?*
- *Which were your least favorite smells? Which objects created those smells?*

OBSERVING/SMELL

Smelly Stickers

Words You Can Use

favorite, odor

What You Need

- various scented stickers
- index cards with labeled pictures of the scented items (cut pictures from grocery-store flyers or print them from a copyright-free Web site)
- chart paper

What You Do

1. Bring in a variety of scented stickers.
2. Have the children smell each sticker and experience the different odors.
3. Ask the children to describe their favorite sticker, the sweetest-smelling sticker, and the most stinky sticker they encountered.

Note: You will have to review the names of odors for young children. They may still have trouble naming them.

4. On the chart paper, list the children's responses to your questions about the stickers, using their exact words.

Questions You Can Ask

- *What was your favorite sticker smell? Why?*
- *What was your least favorite sticker smell? Why?*
- *If you were to create your own sticker smell, what would it be?*

OBSERVING/SMELL

Smelly Jelly Beans

Words You Can Use

jelly bean

What You Need

- variety of jelly beans with distinctive smells
- one plastic bowl for each small group
- napkins

What You Do

1. Prepare ahead by pouring assorted jelly beans into bowls.
2. Separate the children into small groups.
3. Give each group a bowl of jelly beans.
4. Give each child a napkin.
5. Have the children pass the bowls of jelly beans around in their groups.
6. Ask the children to take time to observe the jelly beans by using only their sense of sight.
7. Next, have the children pick up three or four jelly beans, one at a time, and smell each jelly bean.
8. After they smell a jelly bean, have them lay it on their own napkin. The children will notice that not all of the jelly beans smell the same.
9. Now have the children try to guess the flavor of their jelly beans using their sense of smell. Encourage them to discuss their predictions with the other children in their group, explaining why they think the jelly beans are certain flavors.
10. Finally, invite the children to taste one jelly bean at a time to see if the flavor they predicted was correct. Again, encourage them to discuss their findings with their group.
11. Then invite all of the children to share their findings through a whole-group discussion.

Questions You Can Ask

- *What flavors did you decide the jelly beans were by smelling them?*
- *How did the color of the jelly bean help you identify its flavor?*

OBSERVING/SMELL

Look Alike but Smell Different

Words You Can Use

chemist, clear, liquid, waft

What You Need

- two identical clear bottles
- water
- water with peppermint extract
- pictures of chemists, both male and female, from various cultures
- chart paper

What You Do

1. Prepare ahead by filling one clear bottle with water.
2. Fill the other clear bottle with water mixed with peppermint extract.
3. Gather the children.
4. Show the children the two bottles and ask them to describe what they see.
5. Record their various observations on the chart paper.
6. Ask the children questions, such as "Do you think these bottles are filled with the same liquid or not?" "Why do you think the liquids are the same?" "Why do you think they're different?" "What could we do to find out whether they are the same or different?" Usually a child will suggest that smelling the liquid might help, but if not, help the children think of this by sniffing with your nose.
7. Demonstrate the safe way to smell a substance by keeping your face a safe distance from the bottle. Then hold the bottle in one hand, and with the other hand waft the fumes toward your nose.
8. Show the children the pictures of the chemists. Describe chemists and what they do. Explain that real chemists use this procedure in investigating odors.
9. Next, allow each child to smell each of the liquids. Discuss their observations and reactions by asking what they smelled or noticed. Record their observations on the chart paper.
10. Explain that even though they may look alike, the liquids in the bottles are not the same. We can tell whether the liquids are the same or not the same by using our sense of smell.

Questions You Can Ask

- *Were the bottles filled with the same liquid?*
- *How did you know?*
- *Did the bottles smell the same?*
- *What is a chemist? What do chemists do?*
- *How do chemists smell things safely?*
- *How do you think chemists use their sense of smell in their work?*

OBSERVING/SMELL

Look Different but Smell Alike

Words You Can Use

ginger ale, identical

What You Need

- two identical clear bottles
- ginger ale
- red food coloring
- chart paper

What You Do

1. Prepare ahead by filling two identical bottles with ginger ale.
2. Add red food coloring to one bottle of ginger ale.
3. Gather the children together into a group.
4. Show the children the two filled bottles and ask them to describe what they see.
5. Record their observations on chart paper.
6. Ask, "Do you think these bottles might be filled with the same liquid?" "What makes you think they are?" "What makes you think they might not be filled with the same liquid?" Allow time for them to explain their thinking. Then ask, "What could we do to find out?"
7. Demonstrate the safe way to smell a substance by keeping your face a safe distance from the bottle. Then hold the bottle in one hand, and with your other hand waft the fumes toward your nose. (Refer to chemists' use of this procedure from the previous activity.)
8. Now allow each child to smell each of the liquids. Then ask, "What did you smell?" Discuss their observations and reactions.
9. Record their observations on chart paper. Explain that even though the two liquids looked different, the children used their sense of smell to help them determine they were the same.

Questions You Can Ask

- *Did the liquids look the same?*
- *Did the liquids smell alike?*

OBSERVING/SMELL

Can You Tell the Smell?

Words You Can Use

hefting, shaking

What You Need

- various canned foods, such as tuna, chicken, tomatoes, pumpkin, or beans
- can opener
- label poster, made by removing labels from cans and gluing or taping the labels onto chart paper; leave space for comments under each label
- colored markers

What You Do

1 Prepare ahead by numbering or color coding the bottoms of the cans with colored markers.
2. Take the labels off the cans and number or color code the labels to match the numbers or colors you put on the cans. (Do not reveal to the children which labels match which cans until after the experiment is over.)
3. Make a poster of the labels from the cans so the children can use the pictures to guess the contents of the cans. Share the product names on the labels, connecting the words with the pictures.
4. Have the children sit in small groups.
5. Model for them how to safely shake a can by hefting and shaking it with both hands, not by dropping it or throwing it. Model how to safely pass a can to another child by placing it on the floor or desktop and sliding it to her.
6. Supervise as the children heft and shake one marked can at a time.
7. Have the children guess the contents of the cans from their experiences with hefting and shaking them. To guess, the children can tell you the can number or color they think goes under each picture on the label poster.
8. Let the children share why they think each can belongs with each label.
9. Then punch a small hole in each can with a can opener.
10. Now that it is partially opened, model for the children how to pass the can by sliding it along the floor or desktop without lifting it up.
11. Allow the children to pass each can and smell each food item.

more →

12. Have them guess the contents of each can using their sense of smell by matching the number or color on the can to a picture on the label poster. Record these "smelly guesses" in a different color or place on the chart.
13. Let the children share why they now think each can belongs with each label.
14. Write their words on the poster under the cans they are describing.
15. Let the children watch you finish opening each can and matching it to its label. Discuss and share these new findings.

Questions You Can Ask

- *Which foods did you identify by hefting or shaking?*
- *Which foods did you identify by smell?*
- *Which method worked best? Why?*
- *Which cans were more difficult to guess the contents of?*

OBSERVING/SMELL

Creating Fun Smell Cards

Words You Can Use

ingredient, sprinkle

What You Need

- three-by-five-inch index cards
- one small bottle of white glue for each ingredient station
- strong-scented ingredients, such as cinnamon, minced onion, dried banana chips, garlic powder, or onion powder
- small flat trays such as meat-packaging trays, which you could ask your grocer to donate, or shaker-top jars

What You Do

1. Prepare ahead by creating ingredient stations with small amounts of each ingredient on a tray or in a shaker-top jar.
2. Set a stack of index cards at each station. You can write the ingredient name on the back of each card to build word awareness for young children. Glue or tape a picture of the ingredient to the front of the card.
3. For older children, model how to copy the name of the ingredient they want to smell on the back of their own index cards by turning over the card you have already prepared at each station.
4. Gather the children in a group.
5. Let children pick an ingredient station at which to work.
6. Have the children take an index card and place a drop of glue on it.
7. Let them sprinkle a small amount of one of the ingredients on the wet glue.
8. Challenge the children to guess what each ingredient is by using only their sense of smell.
9. Have them check their answer by asking you or by reading the name of the ingredient on the back of the card.
10. Let children rotate to other stations and make two or three more smell cards.

Questions You Can Ask

- *How many smells were you able to guess correctly?*
- *If you were to make another smell card, what smell would it be? Why?*

More You Can Try

Have children bring other ingredients from home to make into smell cards, or they can select other ingredients from the supply table to make into smell cards.

OBSERVING/SMELL

Please Smell the Gifts!

Words You Can Use

bitter, bright, distinct, gift, smell, salty, soapy, sweet

What You Need

- assorted items with distinct smells such as crayons, soap, and popcorn
- index cards with labeled pictures of the scented items (cut pictures from grocery-store flyers or print them from a copyright-free Web site)
- brightly colored wrapping paper such as red, green, or orange
- paper to make "Please smell!" sign
- small boxes
- chart paper

What You Do

1. Prepare ahead by placing each item in a box and wrapping it in brightly colored paper.
2. Place the packages in the center of where the children will gather along with a big sign that reads "Please smell!"

Note: For nonreaders, simply tell the children to smell the packages.

3. Gather the children together into a group.
4. Invite the children to smell each box and tell what they think they smell. For example, they might say, "The blue box smells like popcorn."
5. Write their responses on chart paper.
6. Discuss their responses.
7. After the discussion, open the boxes and allow the children to smell the items again. Discuss their responses once more, including the scent words. Use the scent cards with pictures to review the scent words.

Questions You Can Ask

- *What objects did you smell inside the packages?*
- *Which was your favorite smell?*
- *How did the smells change when the boxes were opened?*
- *If you were to wrap your own package to give to a friend, what object that has a smell would you put inside the package? Why?*

OBSERVING/SMELL

Flavorless Gum

Words You Can Use

aroma, flavor, peppermint, taste

What You Need

- one piece of peppermint gum for each child

What You Do

1. Gather the children together.
2. Have the children open a stick of peppermint gum, but tell them not to place the gum in their mouths yet.
3. Have the children pinch their noses closed with one hand, and put the gum in their mouths with their other hand and begin chewing it.
4. Ask them about the flavor, or taste, of the gum. The children will not be able to taste the peppermint flavor.
5. Have the children stop holding their noses and chew the gum again. This time the children will be able to taste the flavor. Explain that this is because the senses of smell and taste are closely related.

6. Explain to the children that they could not taste the peppermint flavor while holding their noses because its taste comes from its aroma. This is why food is difficult to taste when you have a cold. Your nose is stuffed up when you have a cold, and taste is difficult to determine.

Questions You Can Ask

- *Could you taste the gum when you held your nose? Why not?*
- *Could you taste the gum when you were not holding your nose? Why?*
- *How does your nose help you taste things?*

OBSERVING/TASTE

Vegetable Texture Tasting

Words You Can Use

bland, chewy, cooked, crunchy, flavorful, lumpy, raw, smooth, soft, sweet, texture

What You Need

- cooked and raw vegetables, such as carrots, celery, onions, potatoes, and beans
- index cards with labeled pictures of the food items (cut pictures from grocery-store flyers or print them from a copyright-free Web site)
- spoons, paper plates, and napkins for each child
- chart paper

What You Do

1. Prepare ahead by cooking each of the food items beforehand. Place them in separate containers for serving.
2. Prepare separate containers of the same items in their raw form.
3. Gather the children together. Remind them not to taste the items until directed to do so.
4. Give each child a paper plate, spoon, and napkin.
5. Put one raw and one cooked item on each child's plate.
6. Carefully examine the raw vegetables with the children, noting the characteristics, shape, and texture of each item. Write the children's observations on chart paper.
7. Also examine the cooked vegetables, comparing them to the raw forms. Write the children's observations on chart paper.
8. Next, have the children take a bite of the same vegetable, raw and cooked. Discuss the differences in taste and texture.
9. Write the children's observations on chart paper.
10. Repeat this process with each vegetable. Use the index cards to review vegetable words.

Questions You Can Ask

- *How does the vegetable taste?*
- *How does the vegetable feel in your mouth? What kind of movement is going on in your mouth, with your tongue, teeth, and jaws?*
- *How are the raw and cooked vegetables the same?*
- *How are the raw and cooked vegetables different?*

OBSERVING/TASTE

Taste Look-Alikes

Words You Can Use

paprika, prune, raw, vinegar

What You Need

- foods that look alike, such as raw potato and apple, salt and sugar, water and white vinegar, cola and prune juice, lemon juice and grapefruit juice, red pepper and paprika
- index cards with labeled pictures of the food items (cut pictures from grocery-store flyers or print them from a copyright-free Web site)
- knife
- spoons
- cups
- plates
- toothpicks
- small basket or container for discarded toothpicks
- water
- chart paper

What You Do

1. Prepare ahead by placing each food item in a cup. Items such as potatoes and apples need to be sliced into similar sizes.
2. Place the cups so the similar items are next to one another with a stack of toothpicks nearby.
3. Gather the children and discuss with them that even though some food items may look the same, they may not taste the same.
4. Have the children describe how the similar items look. Write their descriptions on chart paper.
5. Model for the children how to pick up a food item with a toothpick, taste the item, then throw away the toothpick in the small basket or container.
6. Now have the children use the toothpicks to taste the foods that look alike. Discuss their comments and write their observations on chart paper. Encourage the children to use the names of the food items. Refer to the index cards when necessary.
7. Encourage the children to discuss how the foods look similar yet taste different.

Questions You Can Ask

- *Did you discover any differences when you tasted the foods that looked alike?*
- *How does your sense of sight (eyes) make you think the foods will taste alike?*

OBSERVING/TASTE

Classifying Tastes

Words You Can Use

bitter, salty, sour, sweet

What You Need

- variety of food from four different taste groups, such as

salty	**sour**
crackers	sour cream
pretzels	vinegar
salted chips	mustard
salted peanuts	lemons

bitter	**sweet**
radishes	sugar
horseradish	honey
cocoa	jam or jelly
turnips	whipped cream

- index cards with labeled pictures of the food items (cut pictures from grocery-store flyers or print them from a copyright-free Web site)
- four trays labeled "salty," "bitter," "sour," "sweet"
- spoons
- cups
- wastebasket
- chart paper

What You Do

1. Prepare ahead by labeling four trays "salty," "bitter," "sour," and "sweet."
2. Put an assortment of foods items with different tastes in cups, one food item per cup. Be sure to have a balanced mix of salty, bitter, sour, and sweet foods. Place the cups on a table in no particular grouping. Place the spoons near the cups.
3. Gather the children together into a group.
4. Before tasting the food items, ask the children about their experiences with tastes. What taste groups do they already know?
5. Explain to the children there are four basic taste groups: salty, bitter, sour, and sweet.
6. Familiarize the children with the items to be tasted using the index cards to review the food words.

7. Model for the children how to taste a small sample of an item using a spoon. After they taste the food items, children should sort the food by tasting group on the trays labeled "salty," "bitter," "sour," or "sweet."
8. Allow the children to take turns tasting the items and placing each food item on the tray where they think it belongs. When children are finished tasting a food item, have them place their spoons in the wastebasket. Take time to discuss this process and the decisions about where to place the different food items.
9. Discuss with the children that by sorting the food items onto trays labeled with different taste groups, they have classified the food items according to taste.
10. Chart the taste-group discoveries by listing the four taste groups and the foods that belong in each category on chart paper. Use the index cards to help children connect the words on the cards with the words on the chart.

Questions You Can Ask

- *What are the four different taste groups?*
- *Which foods tasted salty?*
- *Which foods tasted bitter?*
- *Which foods tasted sour?*
- *Which foods tasted sweet?*

OBSERVING/TASTE

Fruit-Salad Sensations

Words You Can Use

mixing, mixture, whipped cream

What You Need

- variety of fruits, such as oranges, apples, grapes, and lemons
- whipped cream
- knives
- plastic spoons or toothpicks for each child
- small bowl for each child
- mixing bowl
- serving spoon
- paper plates
- index card labels with the fruits to be tasted and their pictures (cut pictures from grocery-store flyers or print them from a copyright-free Web site)
- index cards labeled with taste category names: "sweet," "sour," "salty," "bitter"
- chart paper
- tape

What You Do

1. Prepare ahead by peeling and dicing the fruit and placing each fruit on a separate paper plate.
2. Gather the children together.
3. Use the index cards to be sure the children know the names of each fruit.
4. Give each child enough plastic spoons or toothpicks to taste each kind of fruit.
5. Have the children taste samples from each of the fruit plates.
6. Discuss how each fruit tastes. Write the four taste categories of "sweet," "sour," "salty," and "bitter" on a piece of chart paper. Tape the index card labels for each fruit under its taste category.
7. Then use the rest of the fruit pieces to make a fruit salad by placing the prepared fruit in the mixing bowl and mixing thoroughly.
8. Allow the children to describe how this fruit salad mixture looks.
9. Put some of the fruit salad in small bowls for the children and add whipped cream if desired.
10. Have the children discuss the difference in taste between the individual fruit pieces and the salad mixture.

Questions You Can Ask

- *Which fruit pieces did you like best? Why?*
- *How did the taste of the individual fruit pieces differ in taste from the salad mixture?*

OBSERVING/TASTE

Pickle Pucker Pick

Words You Can Use

dill, bar graph, sour, sweet

What You Need

- sweet pickles
- sour pickles
- dill pickles
- small paper plates
- napkins
- three index cards labeled "sweet," "sour," "dill"
- chart paper with columns labeled "sweet," "sour," "dill" to create a bar graph

What You Do

1. Prepare ahead by slicing enough sweet, sour, and dill pickles for each child to have one taste of each kind.
2. Place each kind of pickle on a separate plate.
3. Gather the children together.
4. Have the children make observations about the way each of the pickles looks. Write their responses in the appropriate columns on the chart paper.
5. Discuss with the children how some items can look the same but taste different.
6. Have each child taste the pickle slices and decide which one they like the best by pointing to one of the plates.
7. Now place the index cards beside each type of pickle and have the children tell which one they like best by indicating the type of pickle, either sweet, sour, or dill.
8. As the children indicate their choices, use them to create a bar graph showing the children's preferences. Connect the words on the graph to the index cards beside each type of pickle. Take time to explain how the graph shows which pickles were the class's favorite and least favorite, based on the height of each bar, or column.

Questions You Can Ask

- *How did the pickles taste?*
- *Which pickle did you like best?*
- *What was our class's favorite pickle?*

OBSERVING/TASTE

Salt or Sugar?

Words You Can Use

bitter, different, grains, ingredient, salt, similar, sour, sugar, sweet

What You Need

- bowl of salt
- bowl of sugar
- spoons
- napkins
- chart paper
- index cards labeled "salt" and "sugar"

What You Do

1. Prepare ahead by placing salt in one bowl and sugar in another.
2. Place the bowls on a table and gather the children around the table.
3. Give each child two spoons and napkins.
4. Have the children examine both bowls of ingredients. Next, model for the children how to scoop a small amount of each ingredient onto a napkin, keeping the ingredients separated. Then have them spoon a few grains from each bowl onto their napkins and feel the grains.
5. Discuss how the ingredients look alike and feel alike. Write the children's observations on chart paper.
6. Ask the children to predict whether they think the ingredients will taste the same. Why or why not? Write their responses on the chart paper.
7. Now let the children use their spoons to place a small sample of each ingredient onto their napkins, keeping the ingredients separated.
8. Allow the children to taste each ingredient on their napkins by using their spoons or their fingers.
9. Discuss their observations about the taste of each ingredient, and write their responses on the chart paper. Reinforce with the children how things can look similar but taste different. Be sure to use the words "salt" and "sugar," and to refer to the index cards to review these words.

Questions You Can Ask

- *How are the grains of salt and sugar alike?*
- *How are the grains different?*
- *Which grains taste best to you? Why?*

OBSERVING/TASTE

Bread Around the World

Words You Can Use

bagel, croissant, crust, flat, matzoh, pita, rye, tortilla

What You Need

- pita pocket bread
- bagels
- tortillas
- croissants
- matzoh
- French bread
- flat bread
- rye bread
- index cards with labeled pictures of the bread items (cut pictures from grocery-store flyers or print them from a copyright-free Web site)
- knife
- paper plates
- chart paper

What You Do

1. Bring in a variety of breads from around the world, such as those listed above. Other types of bread could be used as well.
2. Gather the children together.
3. Ask them to share all the different kinds of bread they eat at home. Write their responses on chart paper. Encourage them to describe the shape and taste of each bread.
4. Discuss how people around the world enjoy different types of bread.
5. Show the children the variety of breads they will taste, and use the index cards to connect the words and pictures. Lead the children in a discussion of the shape, color, aroma, and size of the different breads. Write the children's observations of the different breads on the chart paper.
6. Let the children observe you cutting the different breads into small pieces. Put the breads on paper plates with their index cards next to them.
7. Have the children taste each bread. Discuss their observations about the taste of each bread and add them to the chart paper.
8. Have the children vote on the bread they think tastes the best.
9. Summarize the results for the children and determine the class's favorite by making a bar graph. Use the index cards to connect the names of the breads to their pictures.

Questions You Can Ask

- *What was your favorite bread?*
- *Why did you like it?*
- *How was it different from the other types of bread?*
- *What was the class's favorite type of bread? The least favorite?*

OBSERVING/TASTE

Taste Tests

Words You Can Use

diced

What You Need

- diced raw potatoes
- diced grapefruit
- diced oranges
- diced raw apples
- diced cheese
- small cups
- five blindfolds, bandanas, or scarves, folded
- napkins

What You Do

1. Dice the food beforehand. Do not let the children see the ingredients ahead of time.
2. Place each of the diced foods into one of the small cups.
3. Select ten children in the class to be active participants in the taste test. Five will be taste testers and five will be taste assistants.
4. Have each taste assistant sit next to a taste tester.
5. Blindfold each of the taste testers.
6. Ask each taste tester to hold his nose so his sense of smell is eliminated in the taste test.
7. Have each taste tester hold out a hand.
8. Have each taste assistant put one piece of food at a time in the hand of the taste tester.
9. Have the taste tester taste the food. (The taste assistant can take the uneaten food from the taste tester using a napkin and put it to the side, if necessary.)
10. After the taste tester has tasted a piece of food, and while still blindfolded, have him tell what he thought it was. After each food is tasted, reveal the actual food.
11. Ask the children to talk about any surprises they may have had regarding the taste test. Ask if any taste testers guessed the correct food. Ask if any taste testers did not guess the correct food. Discuss the results of the taste tests as well as the children's observations.

Questions You Can Ask

- *What was it like tasting food with your eyes closed and while holding your nose?*
- *How do you think holding your nose affected how the food tasted to you?*
- *Did any of your guesses surprise you after you learned what the foods you tasted actually were?*

OBSERVING/TASTE

Tasting Party

Words You Can Use

favorite, flavor, taste

What You Need

- letter to families requesting favorite foods
- children's favorite foods brought from home, cut into bite-sized pieces
- paper plates
- napkins
- chart paper

What You Do

Note: Send letters home to families in advance to let them know about this activity. Explain in the letter that each child is to bring in her favorite food cut into bite-sized pieces. The child should bring enough of the favorite food for all of the children in the class to taste.

1. Gather the children and have them sit at tables with the food they brought from home. Provide each child with a paper plate and napkin. Before children begin passing around their favorite foods, explain to them that as a science experiment, the food must be tasted in order, so no one should begin eating until asked to do so.
2. Have children pass their favorite foods to other children.
3. Ask the children to taste each food at the same time.
4. After the children have tasted each food, have them describe its taste. List the children's descriptions on chart paper.

Questions You Can Ask

- *What were some of the words used in describing the taste of the different foods?*
- *Based on your descriptions, which foods were the sweetest? Saltiest? Crunchiest?*

OBSERVING/TASTE

Smorgasbord Soup

Words You Can Use

dried, seasonings, smorgasbord, stalk

What You Need

- soup pot
- dried vegetable-soup mix
- soup seasonings, such as salt, pepper, rosemary, or seasonings of your choice
- onion, cut into quarters
- potato, peeled and cubed
- celery ribs, cut into one-inch pieces
- can of tomatoes
- canned vegetables brought in by the children, such as corn, peas, or beans
- fresh vegetables brought in by the children, such as carrots, corn, or peppers, cut into one-inch pieces if needed
- water, enough to fill the soup pot
- one small covered container for each child
- one small bowl for each child
- one plastic spoon for each child
- plastic knives
- napkins
- cutting board
- potholders
- large spoon or ladle

What You Do

Note: Send letters home to families in advance to let them know about this activity. Explain in the letter that each child is to bring in a vegetable (fresh or canned) to make Smorgasbord Soup.

Note: You will probably need to bring in the ingredients listed above to add to the soup, in case some children forget to bring in their vegetable.

1. Begin this activity early in the day.
2. Working with small groups, assist each child in cleaning and cutting up his vegetable. Caution: Be sure to follow all safety precautions (see chapter 2). Use plastic knives when possible.

3. With all of the children gathered around, place all of the ingredients in a pot.
4. Cover the pot and start the soup on high.
5. When the soup begins to boil, turn it down to simmer and let it cook slowly throughout the day. Check on the soup periodically, and add water if necessary. Caution: Always use a potholder to remove the lid on the pot.
6. Serve the soup in small bowls at the end of the day. Caution: Remind the children that the soup may be hot from cooking all day. They should try only a small taste at first.
7. Ask for observations as the children look at and eat the soup in their bowls.
8. In a covered container, send home with each child a small serving of soup to share with his family.

Questions You Can Ask

- *What ingredients did we put in the Smorgasbord Soup?*
- *Why is this soup called Smorgasbord Soup?*
- *How did the ingredients change as they cooked all day?*
- *Was the soup cool, warm, or hot to the taste? Why?*
- *How could we change the Smorgasbord Soup the next time?*

OBSERVING/TASTE

Taster's Choice

Words You Can Use

au gratin, baked, boiled, creamed, fried, grilled, hard-boiled, over easy, poached, roasted, sautéed, scalloped, scrambled, simmered, soft-boiled, toasted

What You Need

- one of the following foods: potatoes, eggs, corn, apples, or bread
- cooking utensils
- plates or bowls, depending on the food chosen
- spoons or forks, depending on the food chosen
- napkins
- chart paper

What You Do

1. Select one of the foods listed above.
2. Prepare the selected food in various ways throughout one week. For example, potatoes could be fried, baked, served au gratin, scalloped, or boiled; corn could be boiled, roasted, grilled, creamed, fried, or sautéed.
3. Have the children sample each type of dish after it has been prepared. Write the children's observations and comments on chart paper after they sample each dish.
4. At the end of the week, review the children's comments and have them share which way of preparing the food was their favorite. Write the children's responses on chart paper.

Questions You Can Ask

- *What differences did you observe between the dishes?*
- *How did the food change depending on the way it was prepared?*
- *Which way of preparing the food did you like the best? Why?*
- *Which ways of preparing the food did you like the least? Why?*
- *What other ways could the food be prepared?*

OBSERVING/TASTE

White Taste Test

Words You Can Use

cornstarch, granulated, powdered, texture

What You Need

- flour
- powdered sugar
- salt
- baking soda
- granulated sugar
- cornstarch
- index cards with labeled pictures of the food items (cut pictures from grocery-store flyers or print them from a copyright-free Web site)
- spoons
- napkins
- chart paper
- tape

What You Do

1. Prepare ahead by spooning each of the six white ingredients listed above on separate areas on a napkin for each child. Place a napkin and spoon on a table in front of each child's seat.
2. Gather the children and explain that this is a science experiment. When they sit at the table, they will need to taste each ingredient on their napkins and make careful observations about what they think they are tasting.
3. Model for the children how to taste and carefully observe the flavors by moving your tongue and swishing the ingredient around in your mouth.
4. Allow time for all children to taste each ingredient and discuss their observations.
5. As a group, have the children try to identify the ingredients using only their sense of taste.
6. Tape the labeled pictures of the ingredients to a piece of chart paper. Beneath its picture on the chart paper, record the words children use to describe each ingredient.

Questions You Can Ask

- *If things are the same color and texture, will they taste the same?*
- *How does the color and texture of something help you identify its taste?*
- *How do color and texture make things taste the same? Different?*
- *Which white ingredients could you identify by taste?*
- *Which ones were hard to identify?*

OBSERVING/TOUCH

Fee, Fi, Fo, Fum—What Am I Feeling with My Thumbs?

Words You Can Use

coarse, corners, crystals, curved, fine, grainy, hard, hollow, index finger, irregular, middle finger, pinky finger, ring finger, rough, smooth, soft, texture, thumb

What You Need

- chow mein noodles, macaroni, dry cereal, rock salt, marshmallows, and beans
- index cards with labeled pictures of the food items (cut pictures from grocery-store flyers or print them from a copyright-free Web site)
- one paper lunch bag for every two or three children
- one plastic bowl for each child
- tape
- chart paper

What You Do

1. Prepare ahead by placing samples of the suggested food items in separate paper bags, enough for two or three children to share. Put these aside for now.
2. Place a second sample of each food item in a plastic bowl for all the children to see. Make enough bowls so that children can share yet still get to feel each item.

3. Tape the index cards to a piece of chart paper.
4. Gather the children in small groups of two or three.
5. Show the children the labeled pictures of the food items and practice the words with them.
6. Let all the children touch and explore the items in each bowl using only their thumbs. Encourage them to discuss the experience of touching things with their thumbs only. Encourage descriptive vocabulary. Write the children's descriptions in their own words on the chart paper under the pictures of the items.

7. Then invite the children to use their fingers and thumbs to feel the food items. Let them discuss how this experience feels compared to using only their thumbs. Again, encourage descriptive vocabulary and write their words under the pictures on the chart paper.
8. Next, ask the children to close their eyes and take turns feeling what is inside the bags.
9. Encourage children to match the items in the bags with the items in the bowls without looking inside the bags.
10. Have the children discuss the similarities between the items in the bowls and the items in the bags.
11. Write on the chart paper any additional descriptive words children use.

Questions You Can Ask

- *What did each item feel like? What words can you use to describe how each item felt?*
- *What was it like using only your thumbs to feel the items?*
- *What was it like using your fingers and your thumbs to feel the items?*
- *How did the items feel different from one another?*
- *What items felt similar?*

OBSERVING/TOUCH

Feet are Neat! What's Under the Sheet?

Words You Can Use

block, doll, eggbeater, feet, rolling pin, sifter, spatula, touching

What You Need

- thin blanket or sheet
- kitchen tools, such as a rolling pin, sifter, eggbeater, cake pan, spatula, bowl, ice cream scoop, and straw
- other items such as a doll, block, shoe, stuffed animal, and ball
- index cards with labeled pictures of the items (cut pictures from grocery-store flyers or print them from a copyright-free Web site)
- chart paper

What You Do

1. Gather the children together.
2. Show the children the objects you will be placing under the blanket or sheet. Be sure all of the children can name the objects and can determine which ones are used in the kitchen and which are not. Use the index cards to guide this discussion.
3. Have the children turn around so they won't see where you are putting the objects underneath the blanket or sheet. **Note**: Place the objects around the edge of the blanket or sheet.
4. Tell the children that next they will feel the objects underneath the blanket or sheet with their feet and try to guess what objects they are feeling. Remind the children that some objects are softer than others, so they should feel the objects cautiously. Model for them how to do this from a sitting position by slowly moving your feet over the objects.
5. Now ask the children to remove their shoes and feel the objects under the sheet only with their feet.
6. Have the children touch an object with only their feet and try to identify it. If the children think they know what the object they are feeling with their feet is, have them

more →

share their guesses. If they can't remember the names of some objects, allow them to point to the pictures on the index cards, but also have them practice saying the real names of the objects. Ask why they think they are feeling particular objects.

7. After all the children have felt the different objects, ask them to find the objects they felt beneath the sheet and to identify them as either kitchen tools or not kitchen tools.
8. Determine how well the children were able to identify the objects by touching them with their feet only.
9. Discuss with the children their discoveries about the differences between using their feet to touch things rather than using their hands.
10. Write the children's observations on the chart paper.

Questions You Can Ask

- *What are some things you do with your feet besides using them to walk?*
- *What would you do if you didn't have any sense of touch?*
- *What did it feel like to use your feet instead of your hands to touch things?*
- *Can you identify things as easily with your feet as you can with your hands?*
- *Which objects were you able to identify by touching them with your feet?*

OBSERVING/TOUCH

Exotic Fruits

Words You Can Use

bumpy, fuzzy, prickly, rough, smooth, sticky, texture

What You Need

- exotic fruits, such as mango, papaya, persimmon, pomegranate, or kiwifruit
- index cards with labeled pictures of the fruit (cut pictures from grocery-store flyers or print them from a copyright-free Web site)
- chart paper
- tape
- cutting board
- knife

What You Do

1. Tape the index cards to a piece of chart paper.
2. Display the fruits for children to see.
3. Gather the children and invite them to discuss the color, shape, and size of each piece of fruit. Practice saying the name of each fruit with the children. Use the index cards to help children learn the vocabulary.
4. Next, let the children touch each piece of fruit.
5. Ask the children to describe how the fruits feel, including their surface textures. Write their responses on the chart paper beneath the picture of each fruit.
6. Ask children to predict what they think the fruit will look like and feel like on the inside.
7. Place one piece of fruit on the cutting board and let the children watch you carefully cut it open.
8. Let the children discuss and describe each fruit's inside appearance. Write their descriptions on the chart paper beneath the pictures of the fruit.
9. Discuss how close the children's guesses were to the actual inside appearance of the fruit.
10. Now have the children touch the fruit on the inside and describe how the cut fruit feels. Write these descriptions beneath the pictures of the fruit.
11. Discuss how the fruits are the same or different on the inside and outside. Write on the chart paper any new observations children make.

Questions You Can Ask

- *Did the fruit feel smooth? Bumpy? Fuzzy? Sticky? Rough? Prickly?*
- *What textures did you discover when you felt the outside of the fruit?*
- *Which fruits had the same textures on the inside? On the outside?*
- *What similarities or differences did you notice between the fruits?*
- *Compare the inside and outside of each fruit. What differences did you notice? What similarities did you notice?*

OBSERVING/TOUCH

Salted or Unsalted?

Words You Can Use

salted, unsalted

What You Need

- pairs of salted and unsalted foods, such as salted and unsalted saltine crackers, salted and unsalted fish-shaped crackers, graham crackers, and pretzels
- salt
- paper plates
- cups
- index cards with labeled pictures of the food items (cut pictures from grocery-store flyers or print them from a copyright-free Web site)
- chart paper divided in half, with one side labeled "salted" and the other side labeled "unsalted"

What You Do

1. Prepare ahead by placing a variety of salted and unsalted food items on plates. Make one plate of food for each group.
2. Pour about one-fourth cup of salt in a paper cup. Make one cup for each group.
3. Separate the children into small groups.
4. Share the names of the food items and use the index cards to help children remember the names.
5. Model how to feel the textures of the foods by touching them with your fingers.
6. Give each small group of children a plate with a variety of salted and unsalted food items and a cup of salt.
7. Have each child feel each food item using her fingers.
8. Have each child touch the grains of salt in the cup.
9. Now have the children decide whether each food item has salt in it or not. To help them decide, ask whether they feel any grains of salt on the food items.
10. Record their responses by taping the index cards in the appropriate column on the chart.
11. Discuss the difference in texture between the salted and unsalted items.

Questions You Can Ask

- *What does salt feel like?*
- *What does a food item without salt feel like?*
- *How can you tell by touching a food item whether it has salt in it or not?*

OBSERVING/TOUCH

Shish Kabobs

Words You Can Use

hard, skewer, soft, sticky, temperature

What You Need

- one wooden skewer for each child
- soft food items that can be placed on a skewer, such as marshmallows, grapes, and strawberries
- hard food items such as O-shaped cereal, hard candies with a hole in the center, and small pretzels
- one paper plate for each small group of children
- index cards with labeled pictures of the food items (cut pictures from grocery-store flyers or print them from a copyright-free Web site)
- scissors

What You Do

Caution: As you prepare for this activity, use scissors to clip off the sharp tips of the skewers.

1. Prepare ahead by placing a variety of hard and soft food items on a paper plate, keeping the hard and soft items separate. Make enough plates for each small group of children. Place the plates and skewers on tables where the children will be able to reach them.

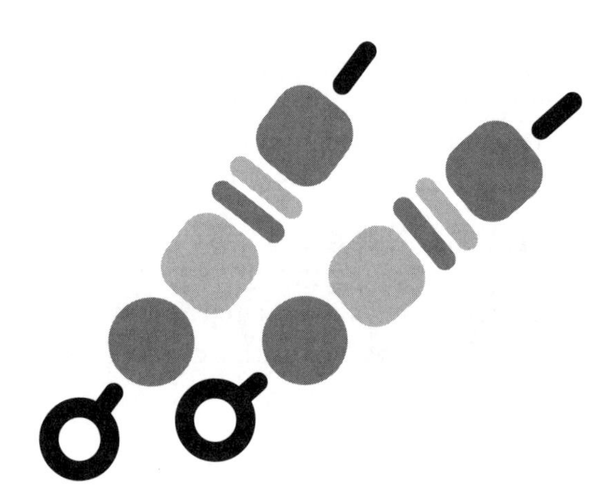

2. Separate the children into small groups and make sure each group has a plate and skewers. Tell the children not to eat the food items at this time.
3. Discuss the names of each food item. Use the index cards to help the children remember the food names. Point out that the foods have different textures, or feel different. Some are soft and some are hard.
4. Show the children a skewer and model how to use it safely by not pointing it at anyone's face or eyes.
5. Model how to put foods on the skewer, alternating between one hard item and one soft item. Tell the children to always begin with a marshmallow to hold the other items in place.
6. Help the children place soft marshmallows on their skewers first, followed by a hard item.

7. Have the children continue putting food items on their skewers in a soft-hard pattern.
8. When the children have finished placing food items on their skewers, check for correct soft-hard patterns.
9. Discuss the differences between the hard and soft textures of the food items. **Note**: Allow children to eat the food items at the conclusion of the activity, if desired.

Questions You Can Ask

- *How did the foods feel in your hands and mouth?*
- *Which food items were soft?*
- *Which food items were hard?*
- *How did you arrange your items on the skewers?*

OBSERVING/TOUCH

This Is So Cool!

Words You Can Use

cool, liquids, sticky, temperature, warm

What You Need

- plastic cups
- various liquids such as water, syrup, soft drinks, milk, or tea (choose two)
- two sheets of poster board
- heat source, such as a microwave or stovetop
- index cards with labeled pictures of the liquids (cut pictures from grocery-store flyers or print them from a copyright-free Web site)

What You Do

1. Prepare ahead by labeling one poster board "warm" and the other "cool." Lay the poster boards flat on a table.
2. Pour the same amount of each liquid (see suggestion above) into two separate cups, to create two sets of liquids. Cool one set by adding ice to each cup or by refrigerating each cup for several hours.
3. Heat the other set of cups until each liquid is warm, but not hot. **Caution**: Stir the liquids, then test them to make sure they are not too hot by dropping a small amount of each liquid on your wrist.
4. Place both sets of cups on the table near the poster boards. Put the index cards next to the appropriate liquids.
5. Gather the children and be sure they know the names of each liquid. Use the index cards to help them remember the names of the liquids.
6. Model for the children how to carefully stick a finger into each cup of liquid and decide if it is cool or warm. Then show them how to place the cup on either the "warm" or "cool" poster board.
7. Now have the children test the liquids themselves and place the cool liquids on the poster board labeled "cool" and the warm liquids on the poster board labeled "warm."
8. Discuss their observations and how they determined whether a liquid was cool or warm.

Questions You Can Ask

- *Which liquids were cool to touch? Which were warm?*
- *How do you know if a liquid is warm or cool?*
- *How do you know which liquids should be kept warm or cool?*
- *How do you know if a liquid should be warm or cool when you eat or drink it?*
- *Which liquids that you drink at home are cool? Which ones are warm?*
- *Which do you like best—cool liquids or warm liquids?*

OBSERVING/TOUCH

You're All Wet!

Words You Can Use

damp, dry, wet

What You Need

- one blindfold, bandana, or scarf for each pair of children
- tub of water for wetting the towels
- one dry towel for each pair of children
- one damp towel for each pair of children
- one wet towel for each pair of children
- one plastic tablecloth or covering for each station to protect the tables
- index cards with labeled pictures of dry, damp, and wet items (cut pictures from grocery-store flyers or print them from a copyright-free Web site)

What You Do

1. Prepare ahead by gathering enough towels for each pair of children to have three.
2. Cover each table with a plastic tablecloth or covering. Set up touching stations for each pair of children with one dry towel, one damp towel, and one wet towel.
3. Have the children work in pairs.
4. Share the labeled pictures as you discuss the meaning of the words "dry," "damp," and "wet."
5. Model for the children how one child in each pair will be blindfolded and will feel each towel, and the other will be the assistant who moves each towel for the blindfolded child to touch.
6. Show the children how to discuss their observations of touching the towels by saying "dry," "damp," or "wet."
7. Have each pair of children move to a touching station with three towels. Now blindfold one child in each pair.
8. Have each assistant move a dry towel, a damp towel, and a wet towel at his touching station for his partner to touch.
9. Have the blindfolded partners feel each towel and say whether it's dry, damp, or wet.
10. When a blindfolded child touches a wet towel, his assistant should say, "You're all wet!"
11. Have the partners reverse roles and repeat the activity.
12. When all the children have had turns touching the towels and being assistants, discuss how they used their sense of touch to feel the differences between dry, damp, and wet. Use the index cards to review these words, if necessary.

Questions You Can Ask

- *How did the three towels feel different from each other?*
- *Which kind of towel felt best to you—the damp, dry, or wet towel?*
- *When would a cool or wet towel feel the best?*
- *When would a warm towel feel the best?*

OBSERVING/TOUCH

Digging for Copper

Words You Can Use

cling, clutch, dig, dusty, grainy, grasp, grip, hard, hold, round, silky, smooth

What You Need

- cornmeal
- copper pennies
- flour
- kitchen utensils, such as mixing spoons, spatulas, or measuring spoons
- index cards with labeled pictures of the kitchen utensils (cut pictures from grocery-store flyers or print them from a copyright-free Web site)
- two plastic tubs
- blindfold, bandana, or scarf
- chart paper

What You Do

1. Prepare ahead by placing some copper pennies in the bottom of the plastic tubs.
2. Next, put cornmeal in one of the plastic tubs and flour in the other tub, making sure to cover the pennies.
3. Gather the children together.
4. Model for the children how you will cover their eyes with a blindfold. Also model how they will feel for hidden pennies in the tubs and describe what they will feel in the tubs while they search for the pennies.
5. Choose one child at a time and cover the child's eyes with a blindfold, bandana, or scarf.
6. Invite the blindfolded children to first dig through the flour tub with their hands to try to locate the pennies. While they are digging, remind them to describe what they are feeling. Write their descriptions on a piece of chart paper. When they find a penny, have them lift it out of the tub and give it to you.
7. After all of the pennies have been found, repeat the activity by placing kitchen utensils in the two tubs and covering them for children to find.
8. Before the children begin searching for the kitchen utensils, use the index cards to help children remember the names of the utensils.
9. While the children dig in the tubs, have them guess which kitchen utensils they think they are feeling.
10. When they find a kitchen utensil, have them lift it out of the tub and name it. Then remove their blindfolds so they can see whether they were correct.

Questions You Can Ask

- *How did the flour feel?*
- *How did the cornmeal feel?*
- *Was it easier to find the pennies or the kitchen utensils?*
- *What kitchen utensil did you find?*

OBSERVING/TOUCH

Some Like It Hot, Some Like It Cold!

Words You Can Use

chilly, cold, condensation, frosty, frozen, heated, hot, icy, temperature, tepid, warm

What You Need

- one bowl of hot water
- one bowl of warm water
- one bowl of cold water
- one bowl with frozen paper towels
- index cards with labeled pictures of hot, warm, and cold items (cut pictures from grocery-store flyers or print them from a copyright-free Web site)

What You Do

1. Prepare ahead by freezing wet paper towels overnight in a plastic bowl. Also freeze a bowl of water overnight.
2. Just before the experiment, make a bowl of hot water by heating water in a microwave. **Caution**: Be careful not to make the water so hot that it might scald or burn a child's skin. Stir the water, feel it with your finger, then drop a small sample on your wrist to check the temperature.
3. Make a bowl of warm water by mixing some of the hot water with cool tap water. Stir and feel it with your finger and wrist, as above.
4. Set all the bowls in the center of the area where you will be gathering the children.
5. Gather the children.
6. Show them the index cards for "hot," "warm," and "cold" as you discuss what these words mean.
7. Model for the children how to put their hands on the sides of a bowl to feel its temperature and say what they think the temperature is—"hot," "warm," or "cold."
8. Now let the children take turns putting their hands on the sides of the bowls to feel the difference in the temperatures. They may have to feel more than one bowl to determine which one is hot, warm, or cold.
9. Have them describe how each bowl feels.
10. Discuss how these words can also relate to temperatures both inside and outside the classroom as well as outdoors.

Questions You Can Ask

- *In addition to feeling the temperature on the outside of the bowls, has the temperature of the water created any other changes such as condensation on the outside of the bowls? Why do you think this might have happened?*
- *What are some other words to describe hot, warm, and cold?*
- *Show me how you feel when you are hot.*
- *Show me how you feel when you are cold.*
- *What kinds of clothes do you wear outside when it's cold? What about when it's hot?*

OBSERVING/TOUCH

Rough and Smooth

Words You Can Use

rough, smooth

What You Need

- fruits and vegetables that are rough and smooth, such as yellow squash, cucumbers, apples, oranges, kiwi fruit, strawberries, grapes, potatoes, and celery
- index cards with labeled pictures of rough and smooth items (cut pictures from grocery-store flyers or print them from a copyright-free Web site)
- chart paper divided in half, with one side labeled "rough" and the other side labeled "smooth"

What You Do

1. Prepare ahead by creating stacks of mixed fruits and vegetables for each group's feeling station, including both rough and smooth food items.
2. Gather the children into small groups at each feeling station.
3. Have them examine the "rough" and "smooth" cards at their stations and discuss what these words mean. Write the children's definitions in the "rough" or "smooth" columns on the chart paper.
4. Have the children set their cards a few inches apart at their station.
5. Model for the children how to carefully feel each item at their feeling stations, and then decide as a group whether it is rough or smooth and place it by the proper card.
6. Encourage the children to explain to each other why they think a fruit or vegetable is rough or smooth. For example, a child might say, "This is rough because I feel bumps" or "This is smooth because it feels slippery."
7. Allow children to take turns sorting their entire stack and explaining their decisions.
8. Finish with a discussion of "rough" and "smooth" and write children's observations of the fruit and vegetables on the chart paper in the appropriate columns.

Questions You Can Ask

- *Which fruits or vegetables did you label "rough"?*
- *Which fruits or vegetables did you label "smooth"?*
- *What does "rough" mean?*
- *What does "smooth" mean?*

OBSERVING/TOUCH

Fine and Coarse

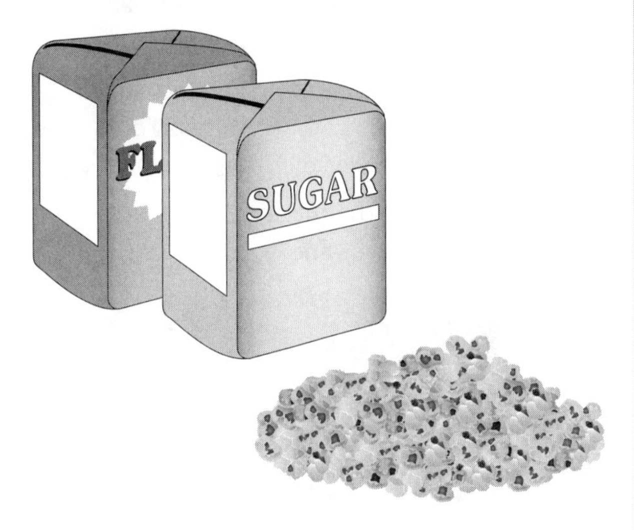

Words You Can Use

coarse, fine

What You Need

- ten clear plastic cups (nine-ounce wide-mouth cups work well), one set of five for each small group
- materials that are coarse, such as rock salt, sand, sugar crystals, granola, rice, popcorn, and dry vegetable-soup mix
- materials that are fine, such as table salt, sugar, flour, cornmeal, flavored gelatin, and pudding mix
- one set of index cards with labeled pictures of fine and coarse items for each group (cut pictures from grocery-store flyers or print them from a copyright-free Web site)
- chart paper divided in half, with one side labeled "coarse" and the other side labeled "fine"

What You Do

1. Prepare ahead by partially filling sets of cups with some materials that are fine and some that are coarse. Put only one material in each cup. Make a feeling station that contains a complete set of the materials for each small group.
2. Create one set of "coarse" and "fine" index cards for each small group, as described above.
3. Gather the children.
4. Show them the index cards, and pass them around as you discuss the pictures and words on each card.
5. Have children share what the pictures tell them about the words "coarse" and "fine."
6. Remind the children that this is a science experiment and that while they are feeling the items in the cups, they should be thinking carefully about how the items feel.
7. Explain that as they feel the items, they should decide whether they are coarse or fine.
8. Model the process of carefully feeling the items in the cups one at a time to decide whether they are coarse or fine.
9. Model how to set the cup containing the item under the card labeled "coarse" or under the card labeled "fine."

more →

10. Encourage the children to think about why they would say that an item is coarse or fine. For example, they might say, "This is coarse because I can feel the little pieces in it" or "This is fine because it feels slippery."
11. Have children gather in small groups to sort the items at the feeling stations.
12. Encourage children to take turns and to discuss why they decided an item was either coarse or fine.
13. Finish with a discussion of "coarse" and "fine," and write the children's observations on the chart paper in the appropriate columns.

Questions You Can Ask

- *Which food items did you consider "coarse"?*
- *Which food items did you consider "fine"?*
- *What does "coarse" mean?*
- *What does "fine" mean?*

OBSERVING/SOUND

Guess the Sound

Words You Can Use

drop, spatula

What You Need

- bowl
- spatula
- sponge
- spoon
- other cooking objects that can be dropped without breaking
- index cards with labeled pictures of the cooking objects (cut pictures from grocery-store flyers or print them from a copyright-free Web site)
- chart paper

What You Do

1. Gather the children together into a group.
2. Show the children the sponge, bowl, spoon, and spatula.
3. Match the index cards to the objects and practice saying the names of the objects with the children.
4. Next, explain that you are going to drop one of the objects, and you want them to see if they can tell what the object is, even when they can't see what you dropped.
5. Explain that when they guess what you dropped, you will ask them why they think it was a certain object.
6. Ask the children to cover or close their eyes.
7. Drop one object.
8. With their eyes still closed, have the children try to guess what you dropped.
9. Ask the children why they think it was a certain object. Their answers might be, "Because the spatula is metal and I heard a clanking sound" or "The bowl is plastic and I heard it bounce." Write the children's answers on a piece of chart paper.
10. Repeat with other objects.
11. As the experiment ends, ask the children to share what they learned about using their sense of hearing, and write their responses on the chart paper.

Questions You Can Ask

- *Which object was the hardest to guess?*
- *Which object was the easiest to guess?*
- *Do all objects make a sound when dropped?*
- *How did sound help you decide what was dropped?*

OBSERVING/SOUND

Having a Band Blast!

Words You Can Use

band, bang, baton, boom, high, kitchen, loud, low, march, music, music director, noise, pitch, play, quiet, rhythm, soft, sound

What You Need

- kitchen utensils that produce sound when they are hit against another object, such as one's leg
- marching band music
- cassette tape player, CD player, or MP3 player
- drawing paper
- crayons
- camera

What You Do

1. Let the children choose a kitchen utensil from those you've collected.
2. Describe how a drum major leads a marching band by raising a baton high in the air and raising his knees high to match the beat of the music. Model this for the children.
3. Have the children take turns being the drum major.
4. Play marching band music and have the children march around the room, keeping time with the music by banging their utensils on their hands or legs. Encourage them to march as if in a marching band, with knees raised high in time with the music.
5. Discuss the rhythm, or beat, of the marching band music, and how all band members must march to the same beat.
6. Play other marching band songs that are faster, slower, softer, louder, and so on. Have children play their kitchen-utensil instruments as they march around the classroom.
7. Take a picture of the "class band" to remember this experience.
8. Let the children draw their own pictures of the "class band" to post to a bulletin board or to send home.

Questions You Can Ask

- *What is your favorite instrument? Why?*
- *What did you do to make your instrument sound louder, softer, faster, or slower?*

OBSERVING/SOUND

What Am I Opening?

Words You Can Use

crunchy, fizzy, guess, tear

What You Need

- brown paper bag
- newspaper
- bottle of a carbonated soft drink
- foam-type food tray from grocery store
- bag of chips
- can of a carbonated soft drink
- bottle opener
- chart paper

What You Do

1. Gather the children together into a group.
2. Show the children each of the objects listed above.
3. Practice saying the names of each item.
4. Have the children cover or close their eyes.
5. Open each item one by one.
6. After each item is opened, have the children guess which object you opened.
7. Ask the children to tell why they thought it was that item. Children can discuss their ideas with other children too.
8. As the experiment ends, have the children share how they used their sense of hearing to decide what items were opened. Write their responses and the words they use to describe the sounds, such as crunchy, fizzy, and crinkly, on the chart paper.

Questions You Can Ask

- *Which object made a tearing sound?*
- *Which object made a rush of air, or fizzy sound?*
- *Which object made a crunchy sound?*
- *How did sound help you decide what was opened?*

OBSERVING/SOUND

Pumpkin Pitch

Words You Can Use

clank, higher, lower, ping, pitch, pumpkin, thud

What You Need

- one pumpkin for each small group
- assorted "instruments" for tapping the pumpkins, such as metal spoons, plastic spoons, ice cream scoops, spatulas (metal and plastic), plastic measuring cups, wire whisks, measuring spoons (metal and plastic), or can openers
- chart paper

What You Do

1. Separate the children into small groups.
2. Give each group a pumpkin.
3. Explain to the children that they will use different things to tap on the pumpkins, and that as they tap, they should listen carefully for the different sounds they make.
4. Model for them how to tap safely on the pumpkins and listen carefully to the sounds, trying to think of words to describe them.
5. Have the children take turns in their groups tapping on the pumpkins using different "instruments."
6. As one child taps, the other children should listen carefully. **Note**: It may be necessary to spread the groups out so they can hear their individual sounds better.
7. As they finish, ask the children to describe the sounds they heard. Write the words children use to describe the sounds on a piece of chart paper.

Questions You Can Ask

- *What kind of sound did your "instrument" make on your pumpkin?*
- *Was it soft or loud?*
- *Which objects made the loudest sounds? The softest?*
- *Which objects made sounds that were alike? Which objects made sounds that were different?*
- *Did any of the instruments make a thud-type sound?*
- *What other words can you use to describe the sound you made when you tapped on your pumpkin?*

OBSERVING/SOUND

What Do You Hear?

Words You Can Use

banging, blowing, clanging, ringing, splashing, swishing

What You Need

- CD of prerecorded sounds or a homemade recording of sounds found in the kitchen or cooking area, such as opening a refrigerator door, using an electric mixer, banging a spoon on the counter, popping toast from a toaster, pouring milk into a glass, shutting a cabinet door, running a smoke vent by a stove, or making a microwave beep or ring
- sound picture cards with a labeled picture of the object that makes the sound (cut the pictures from magazines or print them from a copyright-free Web site)

What You Do

1. Prepare a set of sound picture cards for each small group.
2. Divide the children into small groups.
3. Explain to them that you will be playing a CD of different sounds. Tell them they will need to be very quiet and listen to all the sounds to try to guess where they were recorded.
4. Play one sound and model quiet, careful listening.
5. Then play the whole recording and have children discuss with their groups where they think the sounds were made and why.
6. Allow the small groups to share their thinking with the whole group. Be sure to let them explain why they think as they do.
7. Now give each group a set of sound picture cards.
8. Go over the names of each picture. (You may need to go over the names more than once.)
9. Then have the small groups spread out their pictures so that everyone in the group can see all the pictures.
10. Explain that now they will listen to only one sound at a time, and try to match the sound to one of their pictures.
11. Model for them how to listen carefully and how to pick the picture that matches the sound.
12. Play the recording again, stopping after each sound to allow children to chose the card that matches the sound, until the children have listened to all of the sounds.

more →

13. Allow time for the children to discuss their choices among themselves.
14. Then have children share their discussions and the cards they chose with the whole class.

Note: This experiment could be repeated several times over the coming days.

Questions You Can Ask

- *What sounds did you identify on the CD?*
- *How did you match the sound to its picture?*
- *Which sounds were easy to identify? Which were hard to identify?*
- *In what part of the house are these sounds often heard?*

OBSERVING/SOUND

Matching Sounds

Words You Can Use

alike, identical, match, same, shake

What You Need

- opaque containers with lids, such as film or hosiery containers, food-storage containers, or plastic shoe boxes with lids
- pairs of small kitchen objects, such as bottle caps, measuring spoons, ice-cream sticks, peelers, spatulas, spoons, plastic measuring cups, and wire whisks
- sound picture cards with a labeled picture of the object that makes the sound (cut the pictures from magazines or print them from a copyright-free Web site)
- masking tape

What You Do

1. Make two identical sets of sound picture cards.
2. Prepare ahead by putting single objects in separate containers and closing and taping the lids shut. Make two identical sets of each object. Mix up the containers and set them out at listening stations.
3. Model for the children how to shake and carefully listen to the sound of one container. Then pick up another container, shake it, and decide if the sound matches the sound made by the first container.
4. Ask the children to discuss why they think the sounds match or do not match.
5. If the sounds match, set the paired containers next to each other.
6. Then ask the children to try to guess which object must be in the container by matching it to its sound picture card. Ask them to explain how they know.
7. Next, have the children take turns at each listening center shaking and listening to one container at a time and trying to match it to the sound of another container.
8. When children think they have found matches, let them try to decide which object is in the container by matching it to its sound picture card.
9. Finally, open the containers to see if the children's guesses were right. Discuss their findings. The children should have observed that some objects sound alike and some sound different.

Note: If identifying the objects is too difficult using just pictures, then have a third set of identical objects placed where the children can see them. Children can look at the objects and shake them to match the sounds with the objects.

Questions You Can Ask

- *What kinds of sounds did the objects make?*
- *How could you tell whether objects made the same sounds or not?*
- *How did you decide which objects were in the containers?*
- *Did larger items make louder sounds?*
- *Did smaller items make softer sounds?*

OBSERVING/SOUND

Can-Can Jingles

Words You Can Use

loudest, softest

What You Need

- ten tall potato-chip cans with lids
- wrapping paper in assorted styles and colors
- scissors
- glue
- masking tape
- dry food items such as rice, beans, oatmeal, sugar, spaghetti, peach pits
- macaroni

What You Do

1. Prepare ahead by covering the chip cans with different colors and styles of wrapping paper. Glue the wrapping paper to the cans. Glue a piece of wrapping paper inside the lid to prevent peeking.
2. Fill each can with a different food item from the list above or the same food item in varying amounts.
3. Tape the lids securely on the chip cans.
4. Place the cans on a table in no particular arrangement.
5. Gather the children together into a group.
6. Model for the children how to shake and carefully listen to one can at a time. Then pick up another can, shake it, and listen carefully. As you listen, model how to compare the sounds and place the cans in order from loudest sound to softest sound.
7. As you put the cans in order, explain why you think one can is louder than another.
8. Explain to the children that they will work together to do this with all ten of the cans. (Create only five cans for younger children.)
9. Have the children take turns shaking the cans and listening carefully to the sounds.
10. Have the children decide how to arrange the cans from loudest to softest by shaking, checking, and rearranging as many cans as necessary, adding only one new can at a time.
11. Encourage children to say why they think one can makes a louder sound than the other. **Note**: It may take several guesses and tries at rearranging the cans before the group can decide on a final loudest-to-softest order. The time spent arranging the cans and the conversations surrounding the children's decisions are valuable in developing literacy skills and scientific thinking.

Questions You Can Ask

- *What kinds of sounds did you hear?*
- *Why do you think some cans made louder sounds?*
- *Why do you think some cans made softer sounds?*
- *How did you decide how to put the cans in order by loudest to softest sounds?*

OBSERVING/SOUND

Dropping In

Words You Can Use

banging, clanging, drop

What You Need

- several small food or kitchen items, such as plastic spoons, plastic salt shakers, metal forks, seasoning packages, balls of aluminum foil, small blocks of cheese, or paper cups (one set for each small group of children)
- one opaque plastic or paper shoe box for each small group
- one divider, such as folded poster board or a box lid taped to the desk top for each station
- masking tape

What You Do

1. Prepare ahead by putting several of the small items mentioned above in each shoe box.
2. Create dropping stations on hard surfaces such as tabletops about ten feet apart. Tape a divider in the middle of each station. Place shoe boxes filled with an assortment of the items listed above on one side of each divider. The dividers serve to block the views of the children sitting on opposite sides of them.
3. Separate the class into small groups of two or three children each. Have each group sit at a dropping station.
4. Model for the children how to drop an item from a shoe box without letting the group on the other side of the divider see the item. Also model how they are to be very quiet so the children listening can hear the items being dropped.
5. Encourage the children to say what item you dropped. For example, they might say, "I think that is a paper cup because it didn't sound like it bounced."
6. Now let the children take turns dropping items and guessing what items were dropped. The guessing group has to explain why they guessed certain items. The person who dropped the item can tell the guessing group whether they were right or wrong, and can also keep track of the number of right and wrong guesses. It is okay if children want to allow second guesses.
7. Have children repeat the process for each item, taking turns being the "dropper."
8. After all of the items in the boxes have been guessed, discuss the experiment as a group.

Note: If identifying the items is too difficult, make sets of boxes with identical items inside so all of the groups can see what may be dropped by another group.

Questions You Can Ask

- *How hard was it to identify the items by the sounds they made when they were dropped?*
- *What did you enjoy about this activity?*
- *What kind of sounds did the items make? How many correct sounds did you guess?*

CLASSIFYING

Will It Sink or Float?

Words You Can Use

float, sink

What You Need

- a container with water
- fruits and vegetables, such as bananas, oranges, cucumbers, or carrots; or kitchen objects, such as spatulas, sponges, measuring spoons, or cork stoppers (if using fruits and vegetables, be sure to select a wide variety for the experiment)
- chart paper divided in half, with one side labeled "sink" and the other side labeled "float"
- index cards with labeled pictures of the fruits, vegetables, or kitchen items (cut pictures from grocery-store flyers or print them from a copyright-free Web site)
- drawing paper
- crayons

What You Do

1. Prepare ahead by cutting fruits and vegetables into slices or cubes.
2. Place the fruits and vegetables, kitchen objects, and container of water on a table.
3. Gather the children as a whole group or as small groups.
4. Explain to the children that some objects float in water and some sink.
5. Model for the children how to predict if an object will sink or float, then drop it into the water to check your prediction. If the object sank, tape its picture card in the "sink" column. If the object floated, tape its picture card in the "float" column.
6. Have children take turns predicting which objects will sink and which objects will float in the water, then placing them in the water to test their predictions.
7. Record their findings by taping the index cards in the appropriate columns on the chart. Or children can draw pictures of the objects in the appropriate columns.
8. Discuss their findings.

Questions You Can Ask

- *Which objects floated?*
- *Which objects sank?*
- *Did the size, thickness, or texture of an object determine if it would sink or float?*

CLASSIFYING

Classifying Taste

Words You Can Use

bitter, classify, salty, sour, sweet

What You Need

- laminated mats or food trays labeled "salty," "sweet," "sour," and "bitter"
- a variety of food items to taste that are salty (crackers, pretzels, chips, nuts), sweet (sugar, honey, jam or jelly, sweetened whipped cream), sour (sour cream, vinegar, mustard, lemons), bitter (radishes, cocoa, turnips, watercress)
- index cards with labeled pictures of the food items (cut pictures from grocery-store flyers or print them from a copyright-free Web site)
- chart paper divided into four columns labeled "salty," "sweet," "sour," and "bitter"
- spoons
- cups
- paper plates
- paper bags for collecting used spoons
- tape

What You Do

1. Prepare the food items by placing liquids in paper cups, and slicing fruits and vegetables into bite-sized pieces and putting them on paper plates.
2. Place the cups and plates of food, spoons, and laminated mats on a table.
3. Place paper bags on the table so children can discard their used spoons.
4. Gather the children together.
5. Discuss the four basic tastes: salty, sweet, sour, and bitter. Ask children to name some foods from each taste category.
6. Using the index cards, review the names of the foods to be tasted.
7. Model for the children how to take a piece of food using a fresh spoon. Take a small bite of it and discard the used spoon in a paper bag. After children taste a food, they are to decide if it tastes salty, sweet, sour, or bitter by placing the food on the labeled laminated mat that represents its taste.
8. Allow the children to take turns tasting the different food items and moving each food to the mat where they think it belongs. Tell the children to use a new spoon each time they taste an item. Be sure each child tastes a variety of the foods. Encourage the children to discuss their taste decisions with others.
9. Discuss the children's taste decisions and tape the index cards to the chart paper in the appropriate categories.

Questions You Can Ask

- *Which food items tasted the best to you? Why?*
- *Which ones did not taste good? Why?*
- *Which items tasted salty? Sweet? Sour? Bitter?*

CLASSIFYING

Mixed-Up Madness

Words You Can Use

classify, trail mix

What You Need

- cold cereals with different-shaped cereal pieces such as alphabet pieces and honey-comb-shaped pieces
- trail mix containing items with different shapes and sizes such as pretzels, fish-shaped crackers, and raisins
- two cups for each child
- paper plates

What You Do

1. Prepare ahead by mixing together assorted cereals with various shapes.
2. Pour cereal mixture into cups; make one cup for each child.
3. Pour trail mix into cups; make one cup for each child. **Caution**: Beware of including peanuts, as some children may have peanut allergies.
4. Gather the children together and give each child a small cup of the cereal mix, a small cup of the trail mix, and a paper plate.
5. Discuss that classifying, or sorting, means to separate things by characteristics such as shape, color, and size. Ask the children if they have ever sorted things such as toys or socks.
6. Model for the children how to sort some of the cereal by putting pieces that are the same in some way on a separate part of the paper plate. Show how you decided to sort your items this way.
7. Allow the children to sort their items and discuss their sorting decisions. Older children can sort cereal shaped like letters by vowels or consonants, for example.
8. Have the children share their sorting/classifying choices with the whole group.

Questions You Can Ask

- *How many different piles of trail mix did you sort?*
- *How many different piles of cereal did you sort?*
- *What letters did you find in the alphabet-shaped cereal?*
- *What names did you give your sorted piles?*

CLASSIFYING

Looking at Licorice

Words You Can Use

bitter, licorice, sweet, sour, tart, tangy

What You Need

- variety of licorice flavors, such as traditional black, strawberry, green apple, cherry, grape, and watermelon
- paper plates, one per child and one per small group
- two sets of index cards with labeled pictures of each type of licorice; include the name given by the candy company (cut pictures from grocery-store flyers or print them from a copyright-free Web site)
- tape
- drawing paper
- chart paper

What You Do

1. Prepare ahead by putting a variety of different flavors of licorice cut into one- or two-inch pieces on paper plates, one plate for each small group. Be sure each plate contains several of the same flavor of licorice.
2. Separate the children into small groups and give each group a plate of licorice. Give each child an empty paper plate.
3. Licorice may be a new experience for some children. Ask if any of the children know what they are looking at. Have children share their experiences with licorice.
4. Next, show the index-card label for the traditional black licorice and help children say its name.
5. Then have the children look carefully at the variety of licorice on their group's plate. Remind the children not to eat the licorice yet, because they need to examine it like scientists. Write their observations of each type of licorice on a piece of chart paper by listing each type separately. **Note**: For now, classify their observations by type or color of licorice without naming it specifically.
6. Now invite them to move a piece of each kind of licorice to their own plates and examine the licorice further by touching and smelling it. Again, tell children not to eat the licorice yet.
7. Write the children's new observations on the chart paper. Encourage them to create a name for each kind of licorice based on their observations. Let them be playful with naming the licorice at this point.
8. Now invite them to taste each flavor of licorice. Let them take their time sampling. Write the children's observations of the different tastes on the chart paper.
9. Help them connect the names they gave the different types of licorice to the names given by the candy companies. Share the index cards with the actual names of the licorice and tape each card next to the list describing that licorice.

more →

10. Have children practice saying the names of each type of licorice. Discuss if they think their creative names for the licorice were better than the names the candy companies gave them.
11. Now invite each child to decide on her favorite flavor. Encourage the children to explain why one type tastes better to them than another. Also encourage them to use the real names of the licorice when sharing their preferences, referring to the index cards when necessary.
12. Then have the children vote on their favorite type of licorice. Tally their votes by creating a bar graph on chart paper so the children will have a graphic representation of the class favorites. Space the second set of index cards evenly across the bottom of the paper and tape them to the chart paper. As children vote, indicate each child's vote above the corresponding index card to create vertical bars. After all of the children have voted, share with them how to read a bar graph, explaining that the taller the bar is on the graph, the more popular the licorice is.
13. Discuss the voting results with the class.

Questions You Can Ask

- *How did the look of the licorice tell you what it might taste like?*
- *What was your favorite licorice flavor? Why?*
- *What was your least favorite flavor? Why?*
- *What was our class's favorite flavor?*
- *What was our class's least favorite flavor?*

CLASSIFYING

Rainbow Sort

Words You Can Use

blue, green, least, most, orange, package, red, sort, yellow

What You Need

- one small bag of multicolored, candy-coated, chewy-centered candy for each small group of children
- one paper plate for each group
- index cards labeled with the color words and a sample of each color of candy (glue a candy to each card, if desired)
- chart paper
- tape

What You Do

1. Prepare ahead by cutting open each candy bag then closing it with a clip or clothespin.
2. Separate the children into small groups.
3. Give each group a bag of candy and a paper plate. Remind the children not to eat the candy, because they will be examining it like scientists.
4. Discuss with the children what "sorting" means. Ask if they have ever sorted seashells on the beach, toys, or socks. Let them share their experiences with sorting.
5. Have each group take the clip off their candy bag and pour the candy onto their group's paper plate.

6. Ask for their suggestions on how to sort it. Guide them to agree to sort the candy by color and ask why this might be the best sorting method. (Because color is the only visible difference in the candies at this point.)
7. Have the children sort the candies by color. Encourage them to take turns moving the pieces into piles on their group's plate. If necessary, use the index cards to practice the color words. Remind groups to discuss with each other why they are moving pieces of candy to specific piles, and to use the correct color words.
8. Assist each group's sorting process, if necessary. Ask them why they are making their sorting decisions. Don't just tell them what to do or move the candy pieces for them.
9. After children have sorted the candy, have them count the various colors. Write each group's findings on chart paper and compare the numbers. Tape the index cards

more →

next to the groups' findings, to help children connect the color words to the candy colors.

10. Discuss the sorting process with the whole group.

Note: Because the children have touched the candies, they should not eat them. Have another large bag on hand to divide among the class for a taste test. You can collect further observations by having children taste the various candy colors.

Questions You Can Ask

- *Name the different colors you had in the small bag of candy.*
- *Which colors did you have the most of in your bag?*
- *Which colors did you have the least of in your bag?*
- *Which candy color did the class have the most of?*
- *What is your favorite candy color?*
- *Did all the candy colors taste the same?*

CLASSIFYING

Candy-Worm Wiggle

Words You Can Use

equal, least, fewest, most, sort

What You Need

- large bag of assorted candy worms (enough for each small group to have its own bag)
- paper plates
- plastic bags
- index cards labeled with the color words and the color of each candy (use colored markers)
- tape
- chart paper

What You Do

1. Prepare ahead by making small plastic bags of candy worms in a variety of colors for each group of children.
2. Separate the children into small groups.
3. Discuss the purpose of sorting with the children. Ask if they have ever sorted items such as socks, toys, shells, or crayons. Share their experiences with sorting. Discuss that items in the grocery store are sorted. Ask them if they've noticed that when they go to the produce aisle in the grocery store where the fruits and vegetables are sold that the fruits and vegetables are sorted by type. The apples are all together, the oranges are all together, and so on. Sorting makes it easier for people to find what they need. Discuss other ideas the children may have about the importance of sorting.
4. Give each group a small bag of candy worms and a paper plate. Remind the children not to eat the candy worms, because they are going to examine them like scientists.
5. Ask for their suggestions on how to sort the candy. Guide them to agree to sort it by color and ask why this might be the best sorting method. (Because color is the only visible difference in the candies at this point.)
6. Ask the children to sort their worms by color by stacking them in color piles on their paper plates.
7. Encourage them to take turns moving the pieces into piles on their group's plate. If necessary, use the index cards to practice the color words. Remind groups to discuss with each other why they are moving pieces of candy to each separate pile and to use the correct color words.
8. For fun, tell them to watch to see if the worms wiggle.
9. Assist each group's sorting process, if necessary. Ask them why they are making their sorting decisions. Don't just tell them what to do or move the candy-worm pieces for them.
10. Have the children count the various colors on their plates. Write each group's findings on chart paper and compare the numbers. Tape the index cards next to the

more →

groups' findings, to help children connect the color words to the candy colors.

11. Discuss the sorting process with the whole group.
12. Have the children compare each group of worms and determine which group has the most and the fewest, or if all the groups have the same amount.

Note: Because the children have touched the candies, they should not eat them. Have more candy worms on hand to divide among the class for a taste test. You can collect further observations by having children taste the various colors of candy worms.

Questions You Can Ask

- *How can you tell which pile has the most candy worms? How can you tell which has the least?*
- *Which color pile has the most worms?*
- *Which color pile has the fewest?*
- *How can you tell which piles have equal amounts of candy worms?*
- *Which color piles were equal?*
- *What is your favorite color?*
- *Did the worms wiggle?*
- *Can you make them wiggle more? How?*

CLASSIFYING

Counting Candy

Words You Can Use

classifying, counting, differences, graph, least, most, similarities

What You Need

- large bag of chewy fruit-flavored candy squares
- paper plates
- index cards labeled with the color words and a sample of each color of candy (glue a candy or the candy wrapper to each color card, if desired)
- chart paper
- tape

What You Do

1. Prepare ahead by creating a large vertical bar graph from chart paper to use in classifying and graphing the different candy colors. The graph should be large enough so the children can place the unwrapped candy in its columns. There should be a column to represent each candy color. Place the graph flat on a table.
2. Separate the children into small groups.
3. Give each group an assorted handful of the unwrapped candy squares and a paper plate. Remind the children not to eat the candy, because they are going to examine it like scientists.
4. Discuss what the candy looks like.

5. Ask for their suggestions on how to sort the candy. Guide them to agree to sort it by color and ask why this would be the best sorting method. (Because color is the only visible difference in the candies at this point.)
6. Encourage them to take turns moving the candy pieces into piles on their group's plate. If necessary, use the index cards to practice the color words. Remind groups to discuss with each other why they are moving pieces of candy to each separate pile and to use the correct color words.
7. Assist each group's sorting process, if necessary. Ask them why they are making their sorting decisions. Don't just tell them what to do or move the candy pieces for them.
8. Have the children count the various colors on their plates.
9. Share with the children the bar graph you created for recording their candy-sorting results. Tape the index cards to the top of the columns on the graph to help children connect the color words to the candy colors.

more →

10. Model for the children how to place a candy square on the graph in the corresponding column.
11. Then, have the small groups of children place their candy squares in the corresponding column on the graph. Encourage the children to use the color words as they discuss placing their candies on the graph, referring to the index cards as necessary.
12. While the graph is still on the floor, discuss differences, similarities, and outcomes using the questions below. Be sure to emphasize the color words.
13. Then, show the children how to remove a candy from the graph and color a square in its place to represent the candy, so that you can tape the graph to a wall. Be sure the children understand that doing this does not change the results of the graph. Discuss differences, similarities, and outcomes, again emphasizing the color words. Refer to the index cards as necessary.
14. Discuss the sorting, or classifying, process with the whole group.

Questions You Can Ask

- *How can you tell by looking at the graph which color of candy we had the most of? The least of? The same, or equal, amount of?*
- *Why is a graph useful?*
- *How did the graph change when we moved the candy pieces off of it?*
- *What is your favorite and least favorite color of candy?*

CLASSIFYING

Isn't This Cool?

Words You Can Use

cold, freezer, frozen, refrigerator, sorting

What You Need

- large picture of a refrigerator with a freezer for children to tape pictures on and display on a bulletin board later.

Note: Label the picture so the children see the word for "refrigerator" and the word for "freezer."

- magazine pictures of food that must be kept in the freezer, such as ice cream, frozen pizza, frozen vegetables, canned orange juice, meats
- magazine pictures of food that must be kept in the refrigerator, such as apples, milk, oranges, potatoes, cheese, butter, eggs
- tape

What You Do

1. Prepare ahead by drawing a picture of a refrigerator with a freezer to display on a bulletin board. Make sure it is large enough for the children to tape food pictures on it.
2. Ask the children to share their experiences with foods that should be kept in the freezer and refrigerator. Have them share what might happen to certain foods if they are not kept in a refrigerator or freezer. For example, what might happen to a food that is supposed to be in the freezer but is left out or put in the refrigerator instead? Explain that some food must be frozen to keep it fresh longer or to keep it from melting. Some food is better not frozen and can just be refrigerated to keep it fresh. Freezing some foods ruins them by destroying their texture.
3. Give the children the magazine pictures of food that must be kept either in the refrigerator or the freezer.
4. Have the children sort the pictures into two groups: "keep in the refrigerator" foods and "keep in the freezer" foods. As they sort, encourage them to discuss the reasons behind their decisions. Encourage them to use the names of the foods if they know them as well as the words "refrigerator" and "freezer."
5. Next, assist the children in taping the pictures of food that must be refrigerated on the refrigerator portion of the picture.
6. Assist children in taping the pictures of food that must be kept frozen on the freezer portion of the picture.

Questions You Can Ask

- *Which foods must be kept cold in the refrigerator? Why?*
- *Which foods must be kept frozen in the freezer? Why?*
- *Which foods can be kept in either the refrigerator or the freezer? Why?*

CLASSIFYING

Sorting Seeds

Words You Can Use

different, fruits, seeds, similar, vegetables

What You Need

- variety of fruits and vegetables with big seeds, such as apricots, plums, avocados, acorn squash, pumpkins, corn, sunflowers
- plastic sandwich bags
- paper plates
- plastic bowls or tubs for water (one for each type of seed)
- paper towels
- chart paper
- index cards with labeled pictures of the fruits and vegetables (cut pictures from grocery-store flyers or print them from a copyright-free Web site)
- knife
- cutting board

What You Do

1. Place the fruits and vegetables on a table. Gather the children together.
2. Discuss that the word "similar" means "alike." Ask the children what things about themselves are similar or the same. (They are all children, they go to the same school.) Then ask them what things about themselves are different. (Some have long hair, some have short hair; they are wearing different colors of clothing.)

3. Now see if they can name the fruits and vegetables they will be examining today. Refer to the index cards to help children connect the words with the different fruits and vegetables.
4. Next, let the children watch you cut different fruits and vegetables in half, and have them watch for any seeds. Remind the children of the names of each fruit and vegetable as you cut them.
5. Have the children pick out the seeds.
6. Have the children wash and dry the seeds using the small bowls or tubs of water.
7. Allow the children to discuss the similarities and differences among the various seeds. Remind them to use the correct names of each fruit and vegetable. Tape the index cards across the top of a piece of chart paper to help children connect the words with the pictures on the cards. Write the children's observations of the different seeds beneath the corresponding cards.

8. Then have the children sort the seeds into piles according to seed similarities. Have children put the sorted piles on separate paper plates.
9. Discuss the seeds' similarities and differences. Write the children's observations beneath the picture of the fruit or vegetable from which the seeds came.
10. Place each sorted group of seeds into a different sandwich bag. Pass the bags around for further observations. Review the names of the fruits and vegetables from which the seeds came. Write any additional observations on the chart paper.

Questions You Can Ask

- *How were the seeds similar?*
- *How were the seeds different?*
- *How did we sort the seeds?*
- *What types of fruit were used?*
- *What types of vegetables were used?*
- *What other kinds of seeds could we sort?*

CLASSIFYING

Frozen-Food Frenzy

Words You Can Use

boxes, bread, cartons, cereal, MyPlate, food groups, frozen, fruits, meat, milk, packages, vegetables

What You Need

- a variety of empty boxes, cartons, or packages from frozen foods that represent the food groups from the MyPlate icon (pictures on the packaging should be intact), including items such as carrots, green beans, tomatoes, crackers, macaroni, milk, chicken, strawberries, blueberries, steak, cheese, tuna fish, and rolls
- MyPlate poster from www.choosemyplate.gov/downloads/MyPlate/ColoringSheet.pdf.
- drawing paper
- crayons

What You Do

1. Prepare ahead by collecting empty boxes, cartons, or frozen-food packages that represent the food groups from MyPlate.
2. Divide the children into small groups.
3. Show the children the picture of MyPlate and discuss the different food groups. Give each group samples of the food packages.
4. Model for the children how to look at the MyPlate icon and group the cartons by categories, such as ice cream (dairy group), meat (protein group), vegetables (vegetables group), fruits (fruits group), and so on.
5. Then have each group classify their foods into different groups according to similar attributes. Encourage the children to talk with each other about why they are grouping food certain ways.
6. Discuss the children's findings with the whole group, referring back to the MyPlate poster.
7. Allow the children to draw their own simple MyPlate including pictures of different foods.

Questions You Can Ask

- *What were some of the ways you grouped the foods?*
- *Why do you think we need to eat different kinds of foods?*
- *How could we determine our class's favorite food?*
- *How does MyPlate help us make healthy food choices?*

CLASSIFYING

Cookie Caper

Words You Can Use

bumpy, filled, ingredients, long, plain, round, smooth, unfilled

What You Need

- bags of different types of cookies, such as filled, chocolate-chip, raisin-oatmeal, plain oatmeal, lady fingers, layered, and wafers
- one bowl for each small group
- paper towels
- five paper plates for each small group
- chart paper

What You Do

1. Prepare ahead by putting randomly mixed piles of cookies in a bowl. Make one bowl for each group.
2. Explain to the children that they are getting ready for a party at another teacher's house. She wants her cookies separated, so the children need to help her.
3. Next, divide the children into small groups of three or four.
4. Give each group a bowl of cookies. Explain that for this activity the children will examine and sort the cookies, not eat them.
5. Model for the children how to look at the bowl of cookies and think about how to sort them. Encourage group discussion. For example, a child might say, "I see some that have things in them and some that don't" or "I see cookies that are round and some that are square."
6. Show the children how to sort the cookies into categories and place them all on the same paper plate.
7. Allow the children to sort, discuss, and label their cookie groupings. Be sure children understand that they can sort their cookies in many different ways. They just need to have reasons for their choices, and they need to agree on a name for each category they create.
8. Encourage lots of conversations. Tell children there are no wrong answers for this activity.
9. When the groups have finished sorting their cookies, have each group share its category names with the entire class. Write all of the category names the children came up with on a piece of chart paper.

Questions You Can Ask

- *What cookie category names did you come up with?*
- *How many cookies did you have in each group?*
- *What were your reasons for sorting, or classifying, your cookies the way you did?*
- *Are there other ways you could have sorted your cookies?*

CLASSIFYING

This Is Really Cool!

Words You Can Use

cold, ice, insulated, insulation, uninsulated, warm

What You Need

- large box
- two small boxes with lids
- aluminum foil
- two identical jars with lids
- ice
- newspaper
- lemonade

What You Do

1. Gather the children early in the day. Let the children watch you add ice and lemonade to two identical jars and seal them. Let them touch both jars after a few minutes to see that they are both cold.
2. Now tell them that you are going to create an insulated box. As you work, explain to the children what you are doing at each step.
3. To create the insulated box, lay newspapers approximately three-fourths of an inch thick (two centimeters) in the bottom of the large box. Explain that the newspaper will insulate the box and help prevent hot air (heat) from getting in and cold air from getting out through the bottom of the box. Explain that insulating the box in this way is like putting on a coat to keep warm.
4. Line the inside of one of the smaller boxes with aluminum foil.
5. Place the smaller box inside the larger one.
6. Stuff newspapers between the four sides of the two boxes so that the small box is surrounded by newspaper. Again explain that this will insulate the box some more and help prevent heat from getting in and cold from getting out through the sides of the box.
7. Now let the children feel that both jars of lemonade are still cold. Then place one of the sealed jars of iced lemonade in the small box and cover the box with a lid.
8. Add more newspaper between the lid of the smaller box and the lid of the larger box, and close the lid of the larger box. Ask the children to explain why you added more newspaper between the two lids. The children should be able to tell you that you're adding more newspaper for insulation, to keep the heat from getting in and the cold from getting out through the top of the box. Tell the children you have just finished creating the insulated box.
9. Next, place another sealed jar of lemonade, exactly like the first jar, inside the other small box. This will be the uninsulated box. Be sure the children realize that you are not adding any aluminum foil or newspaper. Ask them to explain why you are not adding any foil or newspaper.

10. Place the boxes side by side in a warm place until snack or lunchtime. (At least an hour should pass before you open the boxes.)
11. Now get the two boxes and open them. Have the children describe the differences they see. Have them feel the differences in temperature between the two jars. Discuss how the paper and the extra box helped insulate one of the boxes by keeping the hot air out and the cold air inside.

Questions You Can Ask

- *Which box kept the lemonade cold? Which box made the lemonade warm?*
- *What other materials besides newspaper and foil could we use as insulators?*
- *What does "insulate" mean?*

CLASSIFYING

Fruit-Kabob Rainbow

Words You Can Use

blue, green, kabob, orange, purple, rainbow, red, skewers, yellow

What You Need

- fruits of different colors and varieties, such as green and purple grapes, cantaloupe, strawberries, blueberries, and pineapple
- index cards with labeled pictures of the different fruit (cut pictures from grocery-store flyers or print them from a copyright-free Web site)
- wooden skewers (snip off the sharp points with scissors)
- toothpicks
- one small paper plate for each child
- one large paper plate for each small group
- napkins
- serving spoon

What You Do

1. Prepare ahead by washing the fruits and cutting them into bite-sized pieces.
2. Put an equal amount of the different fruits on a large paper plate. Make one plate for each small group.
3. Separate the children into small groups.
4. Ask the children to examine their plates of assorted fruits and to discuss with their group how they might sort, or classify, the fruits. Encourage all answers, and have children explain why they would use the sorting methods they suggest.

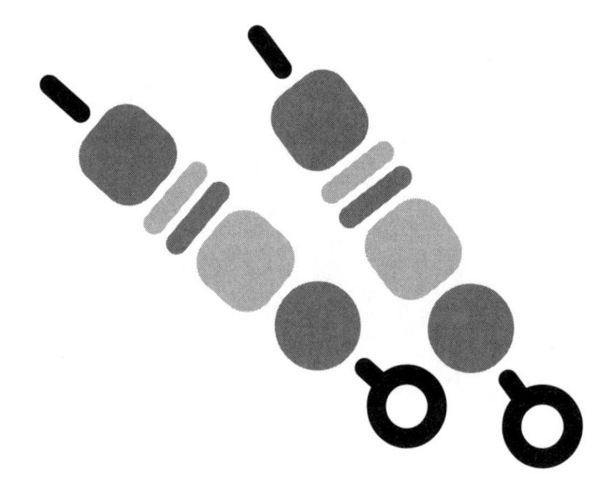

5. Ask the children to name the fruits. Help them by referring to the pictures on the index cards, if necessary.
6. Explain that for this experiment, they will sort the fruits by color.
7. Now give each child a toothpick and have the children take turns moving the fruits around on their group's large paper plate to sort the fruit into color groups. Encourage them to use the color words while they sort and refer to the cards, if needed. Tell the children that they should not touch the fruit with their fingers because later they will be eating the fruit.
8. Then ask each child to take a small plate and put one fruit of each color on it. Show the children the wooden skewers and model for them how to use them safely, by not pointing them at anyone or at their own face and eyes.

9. Model how to put one piece of fruit at a time on a skewer, always holding on to the opposite end.
10. Now give the children their own skewers and guide them in putting their fruits on their skewers.
11. When everyone has finished, discuss the colors again. Using the index cards, review the names of the fruits again.
12. Invite the children to remove the fruit from the skewers and eat it. **Caution**: To prevent children from poking their faces or eyes with the skewers, do not let them eat the fruit directly off the skewers.

Questions You Can Ask

- *What are the different colors on our Fruit-Kabob Rainbows?*
- *What is your favorite color?*
- *What fruits taste best together?*
- *What type of fruit tastes best to you?*

CLASSIFYING

Soak 'Em

Words You Can Use

absorb, colored water, puddles, repel, soak

What You Need

- small items that will absorb and repel water and that will fit in the compartments of an egg carton, such as pieces of cloth, plastic, sponge, wood, apple, cheese, bread, crackers, and sponge cake
- index cards with labeled pictures of the items (cut pictures from grocery-store flyers or print them from a copyright-free Web site)
- one egg carton for each small group
- one eyedropper for each small group
- a small cup of water for each small group
- paper towels
- chart paper divided in half, with one side labeled "absorb" and the other side labeled "repel"

What You Do

1. Prepare ahead by placing in an egg carton an assortment of items like those listed above for each group of two or three children.
2. Gather the children into small groups and explain that for this activity they will find out what things absorb and what things repel water.
3. Ask the children what will happen when you pour water on a paper towel. Then pour water on a paper towel. Ask the children what happened. (The paper towel soaked up the water.) Explain that "soaks up" is what the word "absorb" means.
4. Now ask the children what will happen when you pour water on a piece of plastic. Then pour water on a piece of plastic. Ask the children what happened. (The plastic did not soak up the water—it repelled the water.) Explain that "repel" means "does not soak up."
5. Practice saying the names of the items to be tested by matching the pictures to the words on the cards.
6. Give each small group an egg carton and ask the children to take turns placing one item in each compartment.
7. Give each group an eyedropper and a small cup of water.
8. Have the children use the eyedroppers to put drops of water on each item and notice what happens.
9. Have the children classify the items into two groups, things that absorb water and things that repel water, by placing the index cards in the correct column on the chart paper.

Questions You Can Ask

- *Did some things absorb water better than others?*
- *Which things absorbed the water?*
- *Which things repelled the water?*

CLASSIFYING

I've Been Changed!

Words You Can Use

change, bottom, disappear, dissolve, gone, hold, soft, under, wet

What You Need

- various items that will change when placed under water, such as a dry sponge, liquid soap, a sugar cube, and a teaspoon of salt
- various items that will not change when placed under water, such as rice, peanuts, a spoon, and dried beans
- index cards with labeled pictures of the items (cut pictures from grocery-store flyers or print them from a copyright-free Web site)
- see-through plastic tub
- water
- chart paper divided in half, with one side labeled "things that changed" and the other side labeled "things that did not change"
- tape

What You Do

1. Prepare ahead by gathering a collection of objects. Some of the objects will look different when submerged and some of the objects will look the same when dry and when submerged.
2. Gather the children together into a group.
3. Show them all of the objects and see if they can name each one.
4. Ask a child to hold one of the objects under water for a few seconds.
5. Then have the child remove the object from the water and have another child describe whether the object changed in appearance or not. If the object changed, have the children say, "I've been changed!"
6. Repeat this process for each object.
7. Classify all of the objects by taping their pictures on the chart paper under "things that changed" or "things that did not change."

Questions You Can Ask

- *Which objects changed?*
- *Which objects did not change?*
- *Which objects surprised you by either changing or not changing?*

CLASSIFYING

Make No Beans about It!

Words You Can Use

black bean, garbanzo bean, jar, kidney bean, layer, navy bean, pinto bean

What You Need

- one small plastic peanut butter jar or jelly jar with lid for each small group
- a jar of dried beans layered by type (for teacher only)
- variety of dried beans, such as pinto, navy, kidney, black, and garbanzo
- one small bowl of mixed dried beans for each group
- crayons
- one strip of white paper for each small group (the paper strips should be the same height as the jars)
- clear plastic tape
- large bowl

What You Do

1. Prepare one jar of neatly layered dried beans for yourself.
2. Fill a large bowl with the remaining dried beans.
3. Separate the children into small groups.
4. Give each group a small bowl of mixed beans and a jar with a lid.
5. Have them sort the beans into piles.
6. Show the children your jar of layered beans. Then have the children create their own jars of layered beans by filling their jars to the top with separate layers of different kinds of beans.
7. Model for the children how to tape a strip of paper vertically to the outside of the jar and color it different colors to match the layers of different beans.
8. As a group finishes filling its jar, help the group put on the lid.
9. Tape a strip of white paper to each finished jar and let the children color the paper to match the layers to show that the beans are sorted by type.

Questions You Can Ask

- *How many different kinds of beans did we have?*
- *Which of your layers is the largest? The smallest?*
- *Which is your favorite bean? Why?*
- *What other objects besides beans could we layer in a jar?*

COMMUNICATING

Favorite Juice

Words You Can Use

fruit, graph, juice, rank, recipe, sour, sweet

What You Need

- three varieties of fruit juice, such as apple, grape, and cranberry
- index cards with labeled pictures of the juice varieties (cut pictures from grocery-store flyers or print them from a copyright-free Web site)
- chart paper divided into three columns and labeled with the names of the three juices
- three paper cups for each child
- table to seat all the children

What You Do

1. Prepare ahead by asking your cafeteria manager or cook for samples of three fruit juices they serve. If you do not have a cafeteria, bring in three samples.
2. Pour a sample of each kind of juice into a separate cup for each child.
3. Place all three juice cups at each child's place ahead of time.
4. Gather the children and show them the cups of juice. Remind them not to drink the juice yet, since first they will observe the juice as scientists.
5. Ask the children to share their observations of their three juices. Encourage them to discuss color and smell. Write their observations of the different juices on the chart paper in the corresponding columns, but don't tell them the names of the juices yet.
6. See if they know the names of the juices by their smell. Share the index cards and practice saying the names of the juices.
7. Now have the children sample all three juices. Encourage them to share and discuss the flavors using the correct names of the juices.
8. Explain that "to rank" means "to pick their favorite choice as first, their next favorite as second, and their least favorite as third."
9. Have the children each rank the juices by their first, second, and third choices according to taste preference.
10. On the chart paper, record the children's least and most popular choices.
11. Add a writing experience to this activity by showing the children how to write a drink recipe and follow the sequential steps in preparing a drink. For younger children, this may be in a rebus format, which substitutes pictures for some of the words.

Questions You Can Ask

- *What was our class's favorite juice flavor?*
- *What was our class's least favorite juice flavor?*

COMMUNICATING

Write It Down

Words You Can Use

dairy, frozen, meat, snack, vegetable

What You Need

- paper
- pencils
- chart paper
- marker
- envelopes
- stamps
- journal or notebook

What You Do

1. Prepare ahead by gathering the addresses of local grocery stores, donut shops, or food distributors, as the children will need addresses to write letters to ask how certain foods are grown, processed, made, or sold.
2. Gather the writing supplies.
3. Gather the children together.
4. Discuss what type of food they would like to learn about. Write their responses on a piece of chart paper.
5. Discuss how foods are classified into categories called meats, vegetables, fruits, and dairy, or milk, products.
6. Have the children decide what food item they would like to learn about. They may suggest foods such as corn, peppermint ice cream, gummy bears, donuts, or bananas.
7. Discuss what they want to know about a particular food item and why they want to know more about that food.
8. Next, have them write letters to the local businesses most likely to carry that food. For example, children might write to a local dairy, donut shop, grocery-store produce department, candy factory, or farmer's market. **Note**: For younger children, you will need to write their letters and describe their purpose to the children.
9. In their letters, have the children ask for pictures of and other related information about the food they chose.
10. When the letters are completed, provide envelopes and stamps. You may need to address the envelopes. If the children are old enough, assist them in addressing the envelopes.
11. Add stamps and mail the letters.
12. Monitor the mail and watch for responses. As the responses come in, let each child share with the class the excitement of opening her mail. Lead a discussion of what can be learned from the information received.
13. Then have the children draw pictures of or write in a journal or notebook about the information they learned.

Questions You Can Ask

- *What were some things you learned about the food we studied?*
- *What surprised you about what you learned?*

COMMUNICATING

No Words Allowed

Words You Can Use

beater, flipping, pantomime

What You Need

- index card labeled "pantomime" with a related picture (cut picture from a magazine or print from a copyright-free Web site)

What You Do

1. Gather the children together.
2. Discuss what "pantomime" means. Ask if anyone has any experiences with pantomiming. Explain that "pantomime" means acting out an activity, emotion, object, or action using only bodily movements and facial gestures.
3. Give an example by showing the children how to bounce a ball by moving your hand up and down as if the ball were hitting your hand and bouncing off the floor and back up to your hand. Be sure to change your facial expressions to show how you would feel if you were to miss the ball or make an extra-special bounce.
4. Have children practice saying "pantomime" using the index card to help them remember the word.
5. Discuss with the children how our facial expressions and bodily movements can communicate ideas without using words.
6. Ask the children to think of a cooking activity they have seen. This may include using a beater, flipping pancakes, using a can opener, using a salt or pepper shaker, or using a rolling pin.
7. Have the children take turns pantomiming cooking activities.
8. After each child has had a turn, discuss with the children what they discovered about communicating without words. Encourage the use of the word "pantomime," using the index card to help them remember it.

Questions You Can Ask

- *What was your favorite cooking activity to act out?*
- *What are some other cooking activities that we could act out?*
- *What does "pantomime" mean?*
- *How do we communicate without words?*
- *When have you communicated without words before?*

COMMUNICATING

Are You "Raisinably" Sure?

Words You Can Use

journal, observe, texture

What You Need

- one raisin for each child
- drawing paper
- crayons
- chart paper
- index card labeled "raisin" with a picture of raisins (cut picture from a grocery-store flyer or raisin box, or print from a copy-right-free Web site)
- tape
- one magnifying glass for each child

What You Do

1. Gather the children together.
2. Give each child a raisin, a magnifying glass, and a sheet of paper. Remind children not to eat the raisins, since they will be looking at them like scientists.
3. Have each child carefully observe his raisin using a magnifying glass.
4. Discuss the children's observations, encouraging a focus on color, shape, smell, size, and texture. Write the children's observations of the raisins on a piece of chart paper. Tape the index card to the chart paper.
5. Then have each child draw a picture of what his raisin looks like.
6. Have the children take turns describing their drawings for the group.
7. Discuss similarities and differences in the drawings and in the raisins.

Questions You Can Ask

- *How does a raisin feel?*
- *How does it smell?*
- *What observations did you make of your raisin using a magnifying glass?*
- *How could there be so many differences between raisins?*
- *Where do you think raisins come from?*

COMMUNICATING

Flavor Burst

Words You Can Use

flavor

What You Need

- large bag of chewy, fruit-flavored candy squares
- index cards with labeled pictures of the candy flavors (cut pictures from grocery-store flyers or print them from a copyright-free Web site)
- paper plates
- one blindfold made from a folded bandana or scarf for each pair of children

What You Do

1. Prepare ahead by placing an assortment of different flavors of candies on paper plates. Make one plate for each pair of children.
2. Have the children work in pairs.
3. Discuss with the children that there are different flavors of candies. Let them share the different flavors of candy they have tasted before.
4. Model for the children how one partner in each pair will be blindfolded and will taste a candy and describe what it tastes like without seeing which flavor she is tasting. Be sure to model how the candy to be tasted is picked up and unwrapped by the assistant after the other partner is blindfolded. Remind them that partners will switch roles after the taste test.
5. Give each pair a paper plate filled with the candy assortments.
6. Help the assistants in blindfolding their partners.
7. Let the taste testing begin. Encourage the children to use many descriptive words as they taste a candy, including flavor words such as "lemon," "strawberry," and "orange."
8. After the blindfolded partner has tasted and described the candy, have partners switch roles. Let the other partner be blindfolded and taste a piece of candy and describe it.
9. As a group, discuss the experience using the words for the different flavors tasted. Use the index cards to help with this discussion.

Questions You Can Ask

- *What different flavors of candy did you taste?*
- *Was it difficult to determine the candy flavor without looking at the candy?*

COMMUNICATING

Cut and See

Words You Can Use

clean, cut, draw, observe, windowsill

What You Need

- one banana
- one apple
- a piece of cheese
- one-fourth of a head of iceberg lettuce
- index cards with labeled pictures of the food items (cut pictures from grocery-store flyers or print them from a copyright-free Web site)
- cutting board
- plastic six-ounce see-through cups
- masking tape or labels for the cups (preprinted with the food names)
- knife
- plastic wrap
- water or fruit/vegetable spray
- paper towels
- chart paper
- drawing paper
- crayons

What You Do

1. Prepare the banana, apple, and lettuce ahead by washing them under water or with a fruit/vegetable spray. Cut them and the cheese into small pieces that will fit into the cups.

2. Place each food item into a separate plastic cup labeled with its name.
3. Gather the children together. Explain that they will not be eating the foods, because they will be observing them as scientists.
4. Have the children carefully observe the items, noting color, smell, size, shape, and any other physical characteristics.
5. Have the children draw each food item and label it with its name. Use the index cards to help with this task. You may need to assist younger children with this step, or provide preprinted labels with the food names on them to just peel and stick to the children's drawings.
6. Cover each cup tightly with plastic wrap.
7. Set the items aside on a table or windowsill.
8. Have the children observe the items weekly for two to three weeks.

9. Have them continue to draw pictures of their observations of the food items. Compare each new week's observations and drawings to the previous ones. Share and write the children's observations on chart paper. Use the index cards to remind children of the names of each food.
10. At the end of two to three weeks, discuss the children's findings.
11. Discard the cups of food items.

Questions You Can Ask

- *What changes do you notice about each food item?*
- *What do you notice about the piece of fruit after two weeks? Three weeks?*
- *How does it look or smell different than before?*
- *Why does it look different?*
- *Why do you think these changes happened?*

COMMUNICATING

Question of the Day

Words You Can Use

questions, wonder

What You Need

- chart paper
- markers

What You Do

1. Gather the children for a class discussion.
2. Begin this activity by explaining to the children that some things that happen do make your mind wonder.
3. Explain that when you wonder about something, it causes you to have questions.
4. Then model this by asking questions such as "When did people start putting salt and pepper on their food?" and "Why is there crust around bread?"
5. Solicit answers to your questions and, if children have difficulty coming up with answers, provide possible suggestions.
6. Preface your answers with "maybe" in order to allow the children to see that there may be many different answers and that it is fine to guess.
7. Then, every day at the beginning of class, have children gather for a Question of the Day.
8. During this time, simply ask children to share with the class a question they have that begins with the word "why." Each week, the children can begin their questions with a different word, such as "what," "how," "when," or "who."
9. As a child asks a question, write it on a piece of chart paper.
10. Then try to answer the question as a group, allowing children to share their answers aloud.
11. Focusing on the ways children communicate and explain their ideas, rather than on what's right or wrong, encourages children to give their explanations for their answers.

Questions You Can Ask

- *Ask a variety of "why," "what," "how," "when," and "who" questions about whatever the children come up with that week.*
- *Even though they are not actual questions, have children share "I wonder why . . ." or "I wonder about . . ." types of statements as well.*

COMMUNICATING

What's in the Bag?

Words You Can Use

cool, hard, heavy, light, long, pointed, rough, round, short, skinny, smooth, soft, warm

What You Need

- variety of cooking-related and/or food items children would recognize, such as a spatula, wire whisk, or can opener, a measuring cup, aluminum foil, or a measuring spoon
- paper bags
- tablecloth or piece of fabric

What You Do

1. Prepare ahead by setting out a selection of cooking-related and/or food items covered with a tablecloth or piece of fabric and out of easy sight of the whole group.
2. Gather the children together into a group.
3. Give one child a paper bag.
4. Uncover the items and have the child look at the selection and pick one item to place in the bag, without letting the other children see it.
5. Then have the child describe the attributes of the item, such as "It's long" or "It's round and rough."
6. Have the rest of the children try to guess what the item is.
7. If they are unsuccessful, the child holding the bag provides another clue. This process continues until the item has been guessed correctly or the guesses have all been unsuccessful. Then other children can be given the opportunity to select an item for their bag and provide clues for the other children.

Note: This activity can be integrated with language arts so children can develop a vocabulary of adjectives.

Questions You Can Ask

- *Which items were rough? Hard? Soft? Long?*
- *Which items did we guess correctly?*
- *Which items could we not guess?*
- *What words made it easier to guess items?*
- *What other items could we use next time?*

COMMUNICATING

Fruit and Seed Sculptures

Words You Can Use

collage, edible, flour, fruit, paste, seed

What You Need

- assortment of fruits, such as bananas, oranges, apples, tomatoes, strawberries, grapes, and cherries, all of which are classified as fruits
- assortment of edible nuts and seeds, such as pecans, walnuts, and sunflower seeds
- toothpicks
- flour and water paste, created by mixing flour with water to create the consistency of a thin paste
- small bowls
- construction paper
- water
- plastic knives
- paper plates

What You Do

1. Gather an assortment of fruits. A fruit is anything that contains seeds surrounded by flesh. Start with bananas, oranges, apples, tomatoes, strawberries, grapes, and cherries—all of which are commonly classified as fruits.
2. Separate the children into small groups.
3. Help them cut each fruit open on a paper plate.
4. Now add to the collection some assorted seeds such as walnuts, sunflower seeds, and pecans and other nuts. **Note**: Be cautious using nuts, especially peanuts. Check in advance for allergies among the children.
5. Let the children watch you mix the flour and water paste by adding just enough water to a small bowl of flour so it's the consistency of a thin paste. Share with the children that flour is actually made from the seeds of the wheat plant.
6. Make a bowl of paste for each small group.
7. Guide the children in making sculptures by sticking the fruits and seeds together with toothpicks and some flour and water paste.
8. Ask the children to make up stories about their creations to share with the other children.

Questions You Can Ask

- *Which of these objects is a fruit? A seed?*
- *What materials did you use to make your sculpture?*
- *How many items did you use to make your sculpture?*
- *What different colors are part of your sculpture?*

COMMUNICATING

Tinkering with Tools

Words You Can Use

can opener, eggbeater, grater, kitchen, spatula, whisk

What You Need

- kitchen tools, such as a spatula, eggbeater, grater, can opener, wooden spoon, and bowl
- index cards with labeled pictures of the kitchen tools (cut pictures from grocery-store flyers or print them from a copyright-free Web site)
- chart paper
- tape

What You Do

1. Gather the children together into a group.
2. Place the kitchen tools within easy reach.
3. Allow the children to freely explore and share the kitchen tools. **Note**: Students should be careful handling sharp tools.
4. Share the name of each item by showing its index card.
5. Ask the children how the different tools might be used in the kitchen.
6. Tape the index cards to the chart paper and write the children's responses under each item.

7. Afterward, demonstrate for the children how each kitchen tool is actually used. You may need the bowl to demonstrate this.

Questions You Can Ask

- *How are the kitchen tools like machines?*
- *What other kitchen tools do you or your family members use in the kitchen?*
- *Which kitchen tool is you favorite? Why?*
- *Which kitchen tool makes a sound?*

COMMUNICATING

Chocolate-Chip Cookie Communications

Words You Can Use

brown, bumpy, chocolate, cookie, crumbly, dark, flavor, hard, rough, soft, taste, texture

What You Need

- several chocolate-chip cookies, soft or hard
- plates
- napkins
- chart paper
- one magnifying glass for each child

What You Do

1. Gather the children together into a group. Remind them that for this experiment they will be observing the cookies closely, not eating them (at least not at first).
2. Give each child a chocolate-chip cookie, a plate, a magnifying glass, and a napkin.
3. Using their magnifying glasses, have the children make all the observations they can about their cookies.
4. Ask them to describe their chocolate-chip cookies.
5. Record their responses on the chart paper.
6. Now have them taste their cookies. Add to the chart paper the children's descriptions of how their cookies taste.

Questions You Can Ask

- *What observations did you make about your cookie?*
- *What descriptive words did our class use to describe the cookies?*
- *What makes a good-tasting chocolate-chip cookie?*
- *What is your favorite part of the cookie?*

COMMUNICATING

Advertising Apples

Words You Can Use

apples, core, hard, pulp, round, seed, skinned

What You Need

- red apples
- knives
- napkins
- drawing paper
- crayons

What You Do

1. Have the children work in pairs.
2. Give each pair an apple, a napkin, and a piece of drawing paper.
3. Have partners spend time observing their apples closely.
4. Then have them draw and color a picture of the whole apple.
5. Next, cut each apple in half from top to bottom, giving a half to each child.
6. Have them observe the half apples closely as well.
7. Now have the children draw and color pictures showing the inside of their apples.

Questions You Can Ask

- *What color is the outside of your apple?*
- *What color is the inside of your apple?*
- *What are the brown/black things inside your apple?*
- *Where is the skin of the apple?*
- *What is the shape of your apple?*
- *Is your apple hard or soft?*

MEASURING

Soak It Up!

Words You Can Use

absorb, sponge, soak, tally mark

What You Need

- two small buckets: one half filled, one empty
- one sponge
- chart paper
- water

What You Do

1. Prepare ahead by filling one of the buckets about half full of water.
2. Gather the children together into a group.
3. Model how to submerge the sponge in the water, letting it soak up some water.
4. Now transfer the water by wringing out the sponge into the empty bucket.
5. Show the children how to make a tally mark on a piece of chart paper to count each time the sponge is squeezed out into the empty bucket.

6. Now let the children have turns using the sponge to move the water into the empty bucket.
7. Let the children watch you make a tally mark on the chart paper each time the sponge is squeezed out.

Questions You Can Ask

- *How many times do you think we will have to squeeze out the sponge to move the water from one bucket to the other?*
- *How many times did we squeeze the sponge, moving water from inside the sponge into the other bucket? Let's count the tally marks together.*

MEASURING

How Much Will It Hold?

Words You Can Use

fill, full, measure, pour, volume

What You Need

- water or sand, dried beans or dried peas
- cans of different volumes and different colors or measuring cups of different volumes and different colors
- tub
- chart paper

What You Do

1. Gather the children together into a group.
2. Have children investigate the relationships between the various cup/can sizes by having them answer the following types of questions by measuring.

   Note: The questions will change depending on what color cups you use.

   - How many yellow water cups are needed to fill the green cup?
   - How many green water cups are needed to fill the red cup?
   - How many red water cups are needed to fill the white cup?
3. Record the results on chart paper using drawings of cups that match the color combinations used.
4. Repeat the process with other cup/color combinations. Record the children's guesses and the actual results.

Questions You Can Ask

- *Which of the cups held the most water?*
- *Which cup held the least amount of water?*

MEASURING

Which Is the Heaviest of Them All?

Words You Can Use

heavier, lighter, predict

What You Need

- various cooking and food items, one item per child, such as a potholder, frying pan, orange, apple, or box of gelatin
- index cards with labeled pictures of the cooking and food items (cut pictures from grocery-store flyers or print them from a copyright-free Web site)
- one balance scale for each small group
- paper

Note: The weight of each cooking or food item should not exceed the measuring limit of the balance scales. You will need two items for each child at each weighing station.

What You Do

1. Prepare ahead by setting up weighing stations for each small group with a variety of items to be weighed and a balance scale.
2. Separate the children into small groups.
3. Give each group of children a piece of paper and have them fold it into two parts so they can draw a line in the middle.
4. Have them write "heavier" on one part of the paper and "lighter" on the other part. **Note**: For younger children, you may need to prepare these sheets of paper ahead of time using rebus symbols for "heavier" and "lighter." For example, you could draw a balance scale tipped down for "heavier" and tipped up for "lighter."
5. Model for the children how a balance scale works by showing that the heavier side always goes down whereas the lighter side always goes up, much like a seesaw. Have children share any experiences they've had with seesaws or balance scales. Ask what they think happens when the items on both sides of a balance scale weigh the same.
6. Be sure the children know the names of the items at their weighing stations. Use the index cards to help children review the names.
7. Allow one child in each group to pick up two items.
8. Ask those children to predict the heavier and lighter item by holding the lighter item up and the heavier item down.
9. Tell them to share the items with the rest of their group so that everyone has a chance to predict which item is heavier and which one is lighter.

10. Let children talk about their predictions. Then have them draw the item they think is heavier in the "heavier" column on their papers. Have them draw the item they think is lighter in the "lighter" column on their papers.
11. Next, have children take turns placing both items on the balance scales to test their predictions.
12. Have them discuss the outcome with their group using the names of the items they weighed. The index cards can help with this task.
13. Groups can share their findings with the whole class at the end of the activity.

Questions You Can Ask

- *How did you predict which object would be heavier? Lighter?*
- *For some objects, was it hard to predict which was heavier and which was lighter? What objects were hard to predict? Why?*
- *What was the lightest object?*
- *What was the heaviest object?*

MEASURING

Can You "Bear" It?

Words You Can Use

compare, predict

What You Need

- a variety of cooking or food items such as fruits, vegetables, salt shakers, spatulas, or measuring spoons
- index cards with labeled pictures of the cooking and food items (cut pictures from grocery-store flyers or print them from a copyright-free Web site)
- bags
- one balance scale for each group
- plastic counting bears
- paper
- crayons
- chart paper

What You Do

1. Prepare ahead by putting cooking/food items in bags. Create a bag for each small group.
2. Each group will also need a balance scale, plastic counting bears, paper, and crayons.
3. Separate the children into groups of three or four.
4. Model for the children how a balance scale works by showing them how the heavier side always goes down, whereas the lighter side always goes up, much like a seesaw. Have children share any experiences they've had with seesaws or balance scales. Ask what they think happens when the items on both sides of a balance scale weigh the same.
5. Be sure the children know the names of all the items to be weighed. The index cards can help with this task.
6. Discuss with the children what it means to make a prediction. Ask them if they have ever heard a story and tried to guess the ending or seen a TV show and tried to guess the ending before it was over. Tell them that their guess was a prediction.
7. Model for them how to make a prediction of the number of teddy bears that are equal in weight to an item by picking up the item, picking up one or more teddy bears, and trying to balance the weight of the two in your hands.
8. Then have the children look at one item in their bags and predict the number of teddy bears the item weighs. Have them write down their predictions on paper, or you can write their predictions on chart paper for them. Encourage the children to discuss their predictions using the correct words for the items.
9. Model for them how to check their predictions by putting the item on one end of the balance scale and putting teddy bears on the other end of the scale, until both ends are level. Then tell them that next they would count the number of bears on the

scale and write down that number. (If necessary, you could write the number for them on chart paper.)

10. Now have the children weigh each item to find out the actual number of teddy bears each item weighs. Encourage them to discuss their findings using the right words for each item. The index cards can help with this task.
11. Have the children compare and discuss the differences between their predictions and the actual weight of their items.

Questions You Can Ask

- *How many bears did [name an item] weigh? Ask this question for each object used.*
- *How did you make predictions?*
- *How close were your predictions?*
- *Which object weighed the most in teddy bears? The least?*

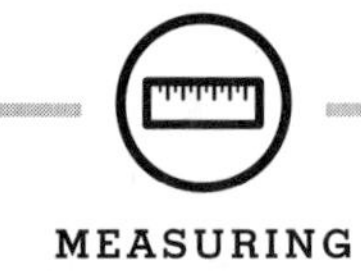

MEASURING

Measuring with Cotton Swabs

Words You Can Use

count, length

What You Need

- various fruits and vegetables, such as green beans, bananas, apples, and squash
- index cards with labeled pictures of the fruits and vegetables (cut pictures from grocery-store flyers or print them from a copyright-free Web site)
- cotton swabs

What You Do

1. Prepare ahead of time a collection of fruits and vegetables for each small group to measure.
2. Make measuring stations for each small group of children that includes fruits and vegetables to be measured and a handful of cotton swabs.
3. Separate the children into small groups.
4. Discuss with them that some things are longer than others, and to compare them. Ask the children if they have ever been measured to see how tall they are. Let them share their experiences with measuring or being measured.
5. Model for the children how to measure length by using cotton swabs. To do this, lay the cotton swabs beside an item, placing the swabs end to end and counting how many swabs equal the length of the item. Express the measurement of cotton swabs in a sentence, for example, "This apple is two cotton swabs long."
6. Be sure the children know all the names of the items at their stations. The index cards can help with this task.
7. Allow the children to take turns measuring the length of each item by laying cotton swabs end to end and counting how many equal the length of the item. As each measurement is completed, the child should tell the measurement of the item to her group. For example, with the banana, the child would say, "My banana is six cotton swabs long."
8. Discuss with the children the results of comparing their predictions with the actual measurement results.

Questions You Can Ask

- *What was the smallest number of cotton swabs you used to measure an item?*
- *What was the highest number of cotton swabs you used to measure an item?*
- *Which object was the longest?*
- *Which object was the shortest?*
- *What other things besides cotton swabs could be used to measure?*

MEASURING

Jelly Bean Balancing

Words You Can Use

balance, guess

What You Need

- one plastic sandwich bag for each small group
- large bag of jelly beans
- one balance scale for each small group
- one apple for each small group
- chart paper
- paper
- crayons

What You Do

1. Prepare ahead by putting several jelly beans into plastic sandwich bags. Make one bag for each small group.
2. Set up a weighing station for each group that includes a bag of jelly beans and a balance scale.
3. Separate the children into small groups. Remind them that the jelly beans are not for eating, because they will be observing the jelly beans as scientists.
4. Ask if the children have had any experiences with jelly beans. Let them share their experiences.
5. Model for the children how a balance scale works by showing them how the heavier side always goes down, whereas the lighter side always goes up, much like a seesaw. Have children share any experiences they've had with seesaws or balance scales. Ask what they think happens when the items on both sides of a balance scale weigh the same.
6. Ask the children to each take out one jelly bean to feel how heavy it is.
7. Now have one child in each group pick up the apple, feel how heavy it is, and pass it to other members of the group so they can each feel how heavy the apple is.
8. Ask the children to guess how many jelly beans it would take to balance one apple on the scale.
9. Have the children record their guesses on their papers, or you can write their guesses on chart paper.
10. Encourage them to share why they think their predictions may be correct.

more →

11. Then have them measure the number of jelly beans it takes to balance an apple by placing the apple on one end of the balance scale and putting jelly beans on the other end until both ends of the scale are even, or balanced.
12. Write each group's findings on the chart paper. Discuss their predictions and the total number of jelly beans it took to equal the weight of the apple.

Question You Can Ask

- *How many jelly beans did it take to balance your group's apple?*
- *Why do you think different groups had different amounts of jelly beans on their balance scales?*
- *Why don't we use jelly beans to measure with every day?*

MEASURING

Lengths of Licorice

Words You Can Use

estimate, licorice

What You Need

- various classroom objects that can be measured
- index cards with labeled pictures of the classroom objects (cut pictures from grocery-store flyers or print them from a copyright-free Web site)
- one licorice stick for each child
- chart paper
- blank self-adhesive labels that can be removed easily

What You Do

1. Prepare ahead by deciding what classroom objects might be easily measured with licorice. Place one label on each object.
2. Gather the children into a large group. Remind them that they will not be eating the licorice at this time, because they will be using it like a scientist uses materials in doing experiments.
3. Discuss with them that some things are longer than others, and to compare them we measure the length of each item. Ask the children if they have ever been measured to see how tall they are. Let them share their experiences with measuring or being measured.

4. Next, ask if they have any experiences with licorice. Let them share their experiences. Explain that today they will be using the licorice in a different way—as a measurement unit.
5. Model for the children how to measure with the length of licorice. To do this, lay the licorice lengthwise on an object. Next, keeping a finger where the licorice ends, pick it up and move it end to end until you reach the end of the object. Count how many times you had to do this to get to the other end of the object you measured. Use a sentence to express the measurement in licorice sticks, for example, "My book is three licorice sticks long." **Note**: Discuss what you want them to do if a measure is not a complete unit of licorice long, but instead is half or one-fourth of a licorice stick. This will depend on the readiness of your group of children to understand partial amounts. You can also have them round up to the next higher number or drop down to the lower number.

more →

6. Give each child a piece of licorice.
7. Have the children observe the length of their licorice.
8. Have them look at the length of the classroom objects that you have identified and have labeled with a sticker. Have them predict how long each object is "in licorice."
9. Then have the children measure and determine the correct number of licorice lengths.
10. Use the licorice lengths to measure other objects around the room and/or school.
11. List some of their findings (measurements) so they can more easily answer the questions below.

Question You Can Ask

- *What did you find around the classroom that was one, two, three, four, five, or greater than five licorice lengths?*
- *How did you use licorice to measure?*

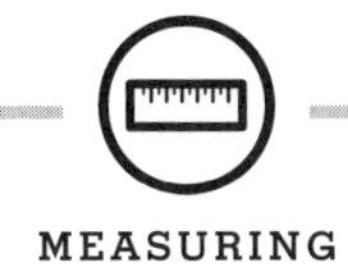

MEASURING

Chocolate and Marshmallow Measuring

Words You Can Use

stirring stick, foam cups

What You Need

- marshmallows
- milk
- chocolate
- one stirring stick for each child
- one foam cup for each child

What You Do

1. Make hot chocolate and pour a cup for each child.
2. Set these cups aside, away from the children.
3. Tell the children that they will be able to drink the chocolate at the end of the activity.

4. Have the children estimate and then measure how many marshmallows it will take to equal the length of a stirring stick.

Questions You Can Ask

- *How many marshmallows does it take to equal the length of a stirring stick?*
- *What was your estimated number?*

MEASURING

Candy-Dust Discovery

Words You Can Use

balance scale, gram mass, measure

What You Need

- one powdered-candy-filled straw for each child
- balance scale
- gram mass cubes (small plastic or wooden cubes that are a cubic centimeter volume and have a mass of about one gram; available in most teacher supply stores)
- small plastic cup, such as those used for liquid medicine
- chart paper

What You Do

1. Gather the children together into a group.
2. Give each child a candy-filled straw. Tell the children not to open them at this time.
3. Using the balance scale, measure the gram mass of the empty plastic cup by putting gram-mass cubes on the scale until it is balanced on each side. Record how many gram-mass cubes it took to balance the scale. **Note**: Mass is the amount of matter in an object. It always stays the same, wherever we are in the universe.
4. Now have the children estimate how much of the plastic cup the candy from a candy-filled straw will fill.
5. Model for the children how to pour the candy from a straw into the cup.
6. Now use the balance scale to measure the gram mass of the cup plus the contents of one candy straw, using the same process as in step 4.
7. Record this data. Compare the gram measure of the cup by itself to the cup with the candy to get a gram-mass measure of just the powdered candy.
8. Ask how many candy-filled straws the children think it will take to fill the cup. Record this guess on a piece of chart paper.
9. Next, cut the top off each candy straw one at a time.
10. Let each child pour the contents of his or her candy straw into the cup. Have the children help you count as they pour. Make tally marks on the chart paper to record how many candy straws it takes to fill the cup.

Question You Can Ask

- *How many grams of candy powder does a candy-filled straw contain?*
- *How many candy straws does it take to fill the cup?*
- *What is the mass of the cup?*
- *What is the mass of the cup plus the powder from one candy straw?*

MEASURING

Baby Bagels

Words You Can Use

bagel

What You Need

- box of round-shaped cereal
- one regular-sized bagel for each pair of children
- small bowls
- chart paper

What You Do

1. Have the children work in pairs.
2. Show them a bagel and a piece of the round cereal.
3. Ask them to guess how many of the small round cereal pieces it will take to fill the center of the bagel. Record their answer on chart paper.
4. Now give each pair of children a bagel and a small bowl of the round cereal pieces.
5. Have the children take turns putting the cereal pieces into the center of the bagel until the hole is filled. Have them count the pieces as they fill the hole.
6. Record their findings.
7. Continue by giving the pairs of children two or three bagels to fill.
8. Let them guess first and then count how many round cereal pieces it will take to fill two bagels and then three bagels.

Questions You Can Ask

- *Why do we call the small round cereal pieces baby bagels?*
- *Do round cereal pieces look like bagels? If so, how?*
- *How many small round cereal pieces does it take to fill the inside of a bagel?*

MEASURING

Pancake Patties

Words You Can Use

pile, stack, utensil

What You Need

- small pancakes, frozen or homemade (enough for each small group to have a stack)
- one kitchen utensil for each child, such as a measuring spoon, egg timer, coffee measuring scoop, tongs, or toddler spoon or fork
- paper plates

What You Do

1. Prepare the pancakes before class. Put several pancakes on plates for each small group.
2. Separate the children into small groups.
3. Remind the children that for this experiment they won't be eating the pancakes.
4. Show the children the kitchen utensils and talk about the names of the items.
5. Model for the children how to stand a utensil up vertically, or on its longest side.
6. Model how to stack the pancakes to equal the length of the kitchen utensil and count the pancakes as you stack them.
7. Give each child a kitchen utensil and a paper plate. Give each group a plate of pancakes.
8. Have the children help each other guess how many pancakes it will take to measure to the top of the utensil.
9. Then have the children stack the pancakes and count the number of pancakes it took to reach the utensil's top.
10. Have the children decide whether their guess was too many, not enough, or just right.

Questions You Can Ask

- *How many pancakes equaled the height of each kitchen utensil?*
- *Did you guess too many pancakes, not enough pancakes, or just the right number of pancakes?*

MEASURING

French-Fry Frenzy

Words You Can Use

baked, container, fried, French fries, mass, scales

What You Need

- French fries for each small group of children
- French-fry container for each small group of children
- small baked potato for each small group of children
- one balance scale for each group
- gram mass cubes (small plastic or wooden cubes that are a cubic centimeter volume and have a mass of about one gram; available in most teacher supply stores)

What You Do

1. Separate the children into small groups and give each group a container of French fries and a balance scale. Remind the children that for this experiment they won't be eating the French fries.
2. Have the groups estimate how many French fries will equal the mass of a small baked potato.
3. Have each group place all the French fries on one end of the balance scale and the small baked potato on the other end of the scale.
4. Allow the children to observe which end of the scale goes down. Which end goes up? Ask them to tell you what they think this means.
5. Explain to the children that the item with the most mass will weigh down its end of the balance scale. If the children have had experiences with seesaws, compare a balance scale to a seesaw.
6. Have the children observe which item has the most mass. **Note**: Mass is the amount of matter in an object. It always stays the same wherever we are in the universe, as compared to weight, which is based on gravitational pull and can change from place to place, such as from the moon to the earth.
7. Now have the children add or remove fries until the scale balances. Have them observe this process closely. Ask what they think this means.

Questions You Can Ask

- *How many French fries do you think it will take to balance the baked potato?*
- *How many French fries did it take to balance your baked potato?*
- *Which has the most mass, the French fries or the potato?*

INFERRING

Sweet as Sugar

Words You Can Use

dissolve, sugar cube, sweet

What You Need

- one clear plastic cup for each child
- water
- one sugar cube for each child
- one stirring stick for each child

What You Do

1. Prepare ahead by pouring some water into a clear plastic cup for each child.
2. Gather the children in a large group.
3. Have each child taste the liquid in his cup.
4. Next, place a sugar cube in each cup of water.
5. Have the children stir the water and sugar using their stirring sticks.
6. Have the children observe what happens.
7. Ask them to infer, or guess, where the sugar went.
8. After giving the children ample time to make inferences, have them taste the liquid.
9. Ask them for their observations again.
10. Explain the word "dissolve" to the children.

Questions You Can Ask

- *Where did the sugar in the water go?*
- *How do you know?*

INFERRING

Mystery Bag

Words You Can Use

infer, mystery

What You Need

- one paper bag for each child
- cooking or food objects, such as a wire whisk, tangerine, grater, peeler, coffee measuring spoon, or tea bag

What You Do

1. Prepare the paper bags with mystery objects inside ahead of time. Put one object in each bag.
2. Gather the children together into a group.
3. Explain to the children that they are going to try to determine what objects are inside the bags without looking in them.
4. Ask the children which of their five senses can best help them determine what is in the bags.
5. Have a child pick up a bag. Ask the children to infer what they think the mystery object is. Encourage them to share their thinking.
6. Have other children pick other bags and repeat the same process.

Questions You Can Ask

- *Which of your five senses did you use to help you guess what was in the bag?*
- *What was inside the bag? Was your guess right?*

INFERRING

Salt and Pepper Mix-Up

Words You Can Use

dissolve, float, infer, mix

What You Need

- salt
- pepper
- spice
- water
- one plastic spoon for each child
- one clear plastic cup for each child
- one small paper plate for each small group

What You Do

1. Prepare ahead by placing a little salt and a little pepper in separate piles on paper plates. Make one plate for each small group. Also have small cups of water for each child.
2. Gather the children into small groups.
3. Have each child wet one finger on each hand by dipping it into a cup of water. Then have each child use their moistened fingers to dip separately in the salt and the pepper to taste these spices. Discuss the children's observations.
4. Next have one child in each group mix the salt and pepper together with a spoon.
5. Now have each child spoon a small amount of the salt-and-pepper mix into her cup of water and stir.
6. Let the children carefully observe what happens. (The salt will dissolve; most of the pepper will float.)
7. Ask the children to infer why the salt and pepper reacted differently in the water.

Questions You Can Ask

- *What happened to the salt when it was added to the water?*
- *What happened to the pepper?*

INFERRING

Impressions

Words You Can Use

impressions, pasta

What You Need

- clay or playdough
- different kinds of pasta, such as spiral, penne, shell, elbow
- index cards labeled with the pasta names and a sample of each type of pasta (glue the samples to the cards)
- chart paper
- crayons

What You Do

1. Prepare ahead by making small impressions in the clay or playdough with various kinds of pasta.
2. Gather the children together into a group.
3. Ask the children to infer how the impressions were made.
4. Allow the children to make drawings of the impressions. Post these drawings on a piece of chart paper or bulletin board under the names of the different kinds of pasta.
5. Show the children how the impressions were made. Give them the opportunity to make similar impressions with the various pasta pieces.

Questions You Can Ask

- *How did the impressions get in the clay/playdough?*
- *Which type of pasta made each of the clay/playdough impressions?*

INFERRING

Foil Cover-Up

Words You Can Use

acorn squash, crookneck squash

What You Need

- cardboard or box lid
- aluminum foil
- a variety of small cooking utensils
- crookneck squash
- acorn squash
- other uniquely shaped foods, such as bananas, artichokes, or spaghetti squash

What You Do

1. Prepare ahead by tightly covering each item with foil so its shape shows.
2. Place the food items on a piece of cardboard or a box lid.
3. Ask children to infer what the item is without unwrapping it or touching it. If using sight alone is too difficult for the children, let them use their sense of touch.
4. For young children, provide a duplicate unwrapped item so they can match it to the one covered with foil.

Questions You Can Ask

- *Were you able to infer what was under the foil through your sense of sight?*
- *What other senses did you need to use? Why?*

INFERRING

Foot Feely Center

Words You Can Use

canned goods, unique

What You Need

- sheet
- variety of uniquely shaped pieces of fruits and vegetables, such as coconuts, pumpkins, watermelons, apples, or longneck squash
- canned goods

What You Do

1. Prepare ahead by placing the canned goods and uniquely shaped foods under a sheet.
2. Have a few children at a time remove their shoes and lightly touch the items hidden under the sheet with their feet. Make sure each child gets a chance to feel with their feet.
3. Have the children infer what the items are based on their observation skill of touch.

Questions You Can Ask

- *Were you able to feel the objects with your feet?*
- *Could you infer what the objects were?*
- *Can you really feel with your feet?*

INFERRING

Dancing Raisins

Words You Can Use

dance, raisins

What You Need

- two small boxes of raisins for each small group
- small plastic cups
- napkins
- any clear carbonated beverage
- drawing paper
- crayons

What You Do

1. Prepare ahead by setting out one plastic cup and a small box of raisins for each group. **Note**: A key element to the success of this activity is the freshness of the drink and the raisins.
2. Separate the children into small groups. Remind them that they are not going to eat or drink the foods at this time, because they will be experimenting with them like scientists.
3. Give each group a small box of raisins and have them observe the raisins. Write the children's observations on chart paper.
4. For each group, pour a cup three-fourths full with the clear carbonated soft drink.
5. Have them sprinkle a few raisins into their cups and observe what happens.
6. Ask the children what the raisins look like in the cups. Write their observations on the chart paper. **Note**: After a while, the raisins will sink to the bottom of the cup. They will stay there for a while and then will rise again. The children should be able to observe the raisins as they begin to dance up and down.
7. Have the children infer why the raisins dance.
8. Tell the children that when the raisins were at the bottom of the cup, they gathered in carbon dioxide bubbles. This is what caused them to float upward to the surface. Once at the top, the bubbles popped and the raisins sank again. This process will happen over and over until the beverage loses its carbonation.

Questions You Can Ask

- *What did the raisins do when you placed them in the soft drink?*
- *Why do you think they did that?*

INFERRING

Celery Soak

Words You Can Use

celery, soak, stalk

What You Need

- two cups
- water
- red and blue food coloring
- two ribs of celery, or as an option, white carnations, daffodils, or other flowers
- index cards with labeled pictures of the celery or flower (cut pictures from grocery-store flyers or print them from a copyright-free Web site)
- napkins
- paper
- crayons

What You Do

1. Prepare ahead by trimming off the bottom end of the celery rib. This will allow for more absorption.
2. Gather the children together. Remind them that they will not be eating the food at this time, because they will be using it as scientists.
3. Be sure children know the name of the food or flower you are using. If needed, refer to the index card to help children remember the object's name.
4. Let the children watch as you put water and several drops of red food coloring into one of the cups.
5. Add water and blue food coloring to the other cup.
6. Put a rib of celery in each cup. Review the process up to now and have the children draw pictures of their observations.
7. Invite the children to infer what they think will happen to the celery sticks.
8. Observe the celery sticks for several days. Let the children make new drawings of the celery or add to their first drawings every few days.
9. After the food coloring has traveled through the celery and reached its top, have the children infer what happened to the dye and the tips of the celery leaves. Discuss the activity findings with them.
10. Try this same activity with white carnations.

Questions You Can Ask

- *Why did the celery leaves turn colors?*
- *How did the food coloring get into the leaves?*
- *How do trees and other plants get their water?*

INFERRING

Make No Bones About It!

Words You Can Use

bones, chicken, joint, skeleton

What You Need

- whole chicken
- picture of a chicken skeleton (if available from a copyright-free Web site)
- bleach
- water
- tub
- paper
- crayons
- chart paper

What You Do

1. Prepare an entire chicken several days ahead by boiling it. Allow the meat to cool and remove as much meat from the bones as you can. **Note**: The longer you boil the chicken, the easier it will be to remove all the bones.
2. Place the chicken bones in a tub of water and add about one-fourth cup of bleach.
3. Allow the bones to soak for a day.
4. Rinse them thoroughly and allow them to dry for at least a day. Now they are ready to use.
5. Bring the chicken bones to class.
6. Gather the children in a circle so they can see the chicken bones.
7. Discuss with the children whether they have ever eaten chicken and what pieces of chicken they have eaten look like. Have them draw pictures of what they remember about chicken that has been eaten.
8. Have the children observe the bones, noting the difference between these chicken bones and ones they remember from chicken they have eaten. Have them note color, texture, and shape. Discuss their observations and write them on a piece of chart paper.
9. Have them infer why these bones are so clean.

Questions You Can Ask

- *How are the chicken bones like our bones?*
- *Why did the chicken bones become so clean after they were soaked?*

INFERRING

Pea Power

Words You Can Use

absorb, gravity, peas, soak

What You Need

- small plastic container with a lid
- dried peas
- saucer
- water
- drawing paper
- crayons

What You Do

1. Gather the children together into a group so they can observe you.
2. Have them watch you fill the small plastic container with dried peas.
3. Place the container on a saucer.
4. Pour cold water to the top of the container to fill it.
5. Place the lid on top of the container of peas and water.
6. Set the container aside until the next day.
7. The next day, have children share their observations of the peas. Let them draw pictures of what they observe.
8. Gather the children the following morning to look at the container of peas. Ask children about their observations, and let them draw pictures of what they now see.
9. Ask them to infer how the lid got pushed off the container.
10. Tell the children that the peas grew big enough to push the lid off the container because they absorbed the water in the container. Dry foods like dried peas soak up a lot of water.

Questions You Can Ask

- *How did the lid come off the top of the container?*
- *Where did the water in the container go?*
- *Why did the peas also fall onto and around the saucer?*

INFERRING

Rubber Eggs

Words You Can Use

rubber, slick, smooth, soft, vinegar

What You Need

- one raw egg (in its shell)
- jar
- bottle of vinegar
- napkins
- crayons
- drawing paper

What You Do

1. Gather the children together around a table.
2. Place the unopened bottle of vinegar, the egg, and the jar on the table.
3. Discuss with the children that some food items have a strong smell, and the vinegar you will use today will have a very strong odor, or smell.
4. Have the children look at the raw egg and share their observations. They may pass it around if you feel this can be done without it being dropped. Caution them about how fragile it is and model for them how to pass it by cupping your hands and letting a child put the egg into your cupped hands.
5. Gently place the raw egg in a jar and cover it with vinegar.
6. Put the lid on the jar and set it aside for about one or two days.
7. Have the children observe the egg each day. Discuss the children's observations and have them draw pictures of what they see.
8. After about two days, the egg shell should be invisible. Have the children discuss their observations and draw pictures.
9. Then, remove the egg, rinse it off, and hold it up to the light.
10. Let the children feel the egg.
11. Have the children infer what happened to the eggshell.
12. Explain that vinegar is an acid and that it dissolved some of the minerals from the eggshell, making the eggshell soft.
13. Have the children discuss the differences between a plain raw egg and an egg that has been soaking in vinegar for three days.

Questions You Can Ask

- *What happened to the eggshell?*
- *How does the egg feel after it has soaked in vinegar for a few days? How does it feel now compared to the way it felt before it soaked in the vinegar?*

PREDICTING

Runaway Droplets

Words You Can Use

absorb, incline

What You Need

- waxed paper
- paper towels
- paper napkins
- paper bags
- plastic wrap
- aluminum foil
- cloth
- oilcloth
- piece of cardboard
- eyedropper or straw
- chart paper

What You Do

1. Prepare ahead by bending a piece of cardboard at an angle to form a ramp. The cardboard should match the size of the paper towel, napkin, paper bag, plastic wrap, aluminum foil, cloth, and oilcloth.
2. Set all the materials on a table. Place the paper towel on the ramp.
3. Gather the children around the ramp.
4. Using an eyedropper or straw, model placing one or two drops of water on the paper towel at the top of the ramp. Ask the children to observe how quickly or slowly the water runs down the ramp.
5. Explain that you have other materials to test how quickly water will run down the ramp. Show the children the different materials and explain that some of them will absorb the water better than others. Ask them to predict which ones will cause the water to run down the ramp quickly and which ones will keep the water from running down the ramp.
6. Write the children's predictions for the different materials on a piece of chart paper. Which ones will absorb the water and keep it from running down the ramp? Which ones won't absorb the water and cause the water to run down the ramp?
7. Next, have the children help test all the materials. Were their predictions correct?

Questions You Can Ask

- *Which material did you think would work best to keep the water from running down the ramp?*
- *Which material absorbed the water droplets the best?*
- *Which materials did not absorb the water droplets but let them run down the ramp?*

PREDICTING

Swelling Raisins

Words You Can Use

dissolve, puffy, swell, wrinkles

What You Need

- raisins
- two eight-ounce plastic cups or other clear containers for each small group of children
- one tub of water for each small group of children
- salt
- water
- spoons
- chart paper
- towels
- paper towels
- paper
- crayons

What You Do

1. Gather the children and divide them into groups of two to four children.
2. Model how to fill a container by submerging it under the water line in the tub, and bringing it back up at an angle to keep as much water in it as possible. Remind the children to be careful not to spill water on the floor. **Note**: Provide towels for each group just in case.
3. Discuss with the children what they know about predicting. Ask if they've ever tried to guess the end of a story or a TV show before it was over. This kind of guessing is called predicting.
4. Have each group fill two plastic cups with water.
5. Have the children add one spoonful of salt to one of the cups and stir until the salt dissolves.
6. Have the children drop some raisins into each cup. Discuss their observations and have them draw pictures.
7. Have children predict what they think will happen to the raisins.
8. Have the children set their cups aside for about one hour.
9. After an hour or so, have the children observe what happened to the raisins. Have them draw pictures of their new observations. The raisins in the plain water will become puffy and lose their wrinkles. The raisins in the salt water will not change at all.
10. Discuss the results.

Questions You Can Ask

- *Did the raisins in the two cups look different?*
- *How did the raisins in the water without salt look?*
- *How did the raisins in the water with salt look different?*

PREDICTING

Freeze!

Words You Can Use

freeze, liquid, teaspoon

What You Need

- eight-ounce paper cups that can be written on
- colored markers
- water
- salt
- tray for carrying cups to the freezer
- freezer
- chart paper

What You Do

1. Separate the children into small groups, and assign a number to each group.
2. Give each group of children two paper cups. Write the group's number on the outside of each of its cups.
3. Fill one cup with plain water and label it plain water.
4. Fill the other cup with water and mix in three spoonfuls of salt to create salt water. Label it saltwater.
5. Place all of the cups in a freezer and allow them to begin freezing.
6. Have the children predict which cup of water will freeze first—salt or plain water.
7. Check on the freezing water every hour or so and show each group of children both cups. You may need an adult partner to help with this task.
8. Once a group's cup has frozen, record the time it took to freeze. Record each group's freezing time for both of its cups.
9. Determine which cup froze first.

Questions You Can Ask

- *Which cup of water do you think will freeze first? Why?*
- *Which cup of water actually did freeze first?*

PREDICTING

Colored-Candy Predicting

Words You Can Use

cherry, flavor, lime, strawberry, watermelon

What You Need

- unwrapped colored candy
- clear bowls

What You Do

1. Divide the children into small groups.
2. Put a variety of pieces of colored candy into the clear bowls for each group.
3. Have the children observe that there are several different colors of candy.
4. Have the children predict the flavor of the candy—for example, watermelon, strawberry, cherry, lime, and so on—by simply looking at the candy's color.
5. Allow the children to taste the candy pieces.
6. Have them decide if any of their predictions were correct.

Questions You Can Ask

- *Were any of your predictions correct? If so, which ones?*
- *If not, which ones were not correct?*
- *Which candies looked to be one flavor but turned out to be another flavor? Why was that?*

PREDICTING

Animal-Cracker Predicting

Words You Can Use

animal, crackers

What You Need

- resealable, clear plastic bags
- animal crackers
- napkins
- paper plates
- peel-and-stick labels
- marker

What You Do

1. Prepare ahead by placing different amounts of animal crackers inside several plastic bags and sealing them.
2. Gather the children into a large group. Remind them that they are not going to eat the crackers, because they are experimenting with them like scientists.
3. Ask them to predict which bag has the least amount of or fewest animal crackers in it. Which do they predict has the most? Ask them to explain their thinking.
4. Have the children place the bags in order from fewest animal crackers to most animal crackers.
5. Number the order of the bags by writing their rank numbers on labels and attaching a label to each bag.
6. Give pairs of children a bag and a paper plate. Have the children take out the crackers one at a time and count them.
7. Help them put another label on the bag showing how many crackers it held.
8. Now let the children help arrange the bags from most animal crackers to fewest animal crackers.
9. Compare the original order of the bags to the revised order.
10. Ask the children to share their thoughts on the findings.

Questions You Can Ask

- *Can you tell by just looking which bag has the fewest crackers and which has the most?*
- *How close were your predictions to the actual number in each bag?*
- *How many crackers were in the bag with the fewest crackers?*
- *How many crackers were in the bag with the most crackers?*

PREDICTING

Exactly What Color?

Words You Can Use

beets, coffee grounds, dye, eggs, onions, orange rind, spinach

What You Need

- three or four eggs for each small group of children
- beet juice
- coffee grounds
- orange rind
- spinach leaves
- onion skins
- paper plates
- salt and pepper
- five pots
- potholder
- hot plate
- drawing paper
- crayons

What You Do

1. Separate the children into five small groups.
2. Let the children watch as you place two or three eggs in each pot. Next, place spinach leaves, which will serve as a dyeing agent, in one of the pots. Then, put two or three eggs in a pot with some onion skins. Do this until all five pots are filled with eggs and a dyeing agent. Reserve some of the dyeing agents to discuss at the end of the experiment. Set a pot with eggs by each group of children.
3. Ask the children to predict what color the eggs in each pot will become.
4. Microwave or heat each pot of eggs until the water is hot.
5. Remove the eggs, rinse, and cool. **Note**: As you remove the eggs from the pots, record which pot created which color of egg, but do not share this information with the children yet.
6. Ask the children to identify the food used to make each color of egg.
7. Then show the children which food colored which egg by placing the egg next to the food used to color it.
8. Allow the children to discuss this experiment, and then have them draw pictures to record their thoughts about the experiment.
9. Allow the children to peel the eggs and place them on paper plates. You or another adult can slice the eggs into quarters for the children to eat. Every child should have the opportunity to taste several different versions of the boiled eggs.

Questions You Can Ask

- *Were any of your color predictions correct? If so, which ones?*
- *After you peeled the eggs, did you notice if any of the colors soaked through to the egg?*
- *How did the eggs taste?*

PREDICTING

Cereal Skewers

Words You Can Use

full, skewer, slide

What You Need

- one cup of small, round-shaped cereal pieces for each small group of children
- one skewer or toothpick for each child
- paper towels
- one bowl for each small group
- drawing paper
- crayons

What You Do

Caution: Use scissors to clip off the tips of the skewers or toothpicks as you prepare for this activity.

1. Separate the children into small groups. Give each group a bowl of cereal. Give each child a skewer and a paper towel.
2. Remind the children that they are not to eat the cereal.
3. Have them predict how many cereal pieces it will take to fill up their skewers. Then have them take that many pieces of cereal out of their group bowl and put them on their own paper towel. For younger children, use toothpicks instead of the long skewers.
4. Model for the children how to hold one end of the skewer with one hand while putting the cereal on the skewer with the other hand. Also model how to count the cereal when the skewer is full by laying the skewer down.
5. Next, have the children slide cereal pieces onto their skewers one at a time.
6. Have them slide cereal onto their skewers until they are full. They may have to get more cereal out of the bowl.
7. When their skewers are full, ask the children to lay their skewers down and count the number of pieces on their skewers.
8. Have the children compare their prediction with the actual amount.
9. Let them draw pictures of what they remember from this experiment as a way to reflect on the process.

Questions You Can Ask

- *Was your prediction close?*
- *Did you have leftover cereal? What does this mean?*
- *Did you have to get more cereal out of the bowl? What does this mean?*
- *How many round cereal pieces did it take to fill your skewer?*

PREDICTING

Pizza Pizzazz

Words You Can Use

Italian sausage, pepperoni, sausage balls

What You Need

- Italian sausage balls
- mini cheese pizzas
- napkins
- paper plates
- pepperoni slices

What You Do

1. Prepare mini pizzas ahead of time or buy mini cheese pizzas.
2. Bake them completely in an oven or microwave and let them cool.
3. Cook the Italian sausage balls until they are done.
4. Have the children wash their hands, then gather them together into a group.
5. Pass out a pizza to each child. Remind the children not to eat their pizza at this time. Provide several small bowls with sausage balls and several with pepperoni slices.
6. Have the children predict how many sausage balls and/or pepperoni slices it will take to fully cover up their pizzas. Demonstrate for the children what "fully" means. Encourage children to discuss their predictions.
7. Then have the children fill their pizzas with the sausage or pepperoni slices.
8. Ask the children to count how many pieces were actually needed to fill the pizza.
9. Discuss the results of this experiment.
10. After the activity, invite the children to have a Pizza Pizzazz Party and eat their pizzas.

Questions You Can Ask

- *How many sausage balls and/or pepperoni slices did it take to fill up your cheese pizza?*
- *Was your prediction close to the actual amount needed? Why or why not?*

PREDICTING

Fruit and Vegetables: Sink or Float?

Words You Can Use

float, sink

What You Need

- see-through plastic tub
- variety of fruits and vegetables, such as bananas, apples, lemons, limes, strawberries, mangos, kiwi fruit, papayas, celery, potatoes, peppers, okra, or onions
- water
- napkins

What You Do

1. Fill the see-through tub with water.
2. Hold up each fruit or vegetable and have the children predict whether it will sink or float in the tub of water. Be sure to practice saying the names of the fruits and vegetables.

3. Say the name of each fruit or vegetable as you place it in the water. Have the children observe whether it floated or sank.
4. Discuss with the children why certain fruits and vegetables either sank or floated.

Questions You Can Ask

- *Which of the fruits and vegetables sank? Why?*
- *Which of the fruits and vegetables floated? Why?*

PREDICTING

Carton and Container Predicting

Words You Can Use

carton, pour

What You Need

- three or four small, empty milk cartons for each child
- several easy-to-pour, plastic containers (of various sizes) for each small group of children
- large tub of water for each small group of children

What You Do

1. Prepare ahead by filling a tub of water for each group of children.
2. Gather the children into small groups.
3. Give each child three or four small, empty milk cartons.
4. Have them observe the size of each carton.
5. Give each small group of children several plastic containers.
6. Have the children predict how many small milk cartons it will take to fill one of the plastic containers.
7. Model for the children how to fill their milk cartons by dipping them into the tub of water and then carefully pouring the water into the plastic container. Remind them to count each time they pour.
8. Now have the children pour water from the small milk cartons into the other plastic containers and count each time they pour.
9. Discuss with the children how accurate their predictions were.

Questions You Can Ask

- *How many small milk cartons of water did it take to fill your smallest plastic container? What about the largest plastic container?*
- *Was your prediction correct or not?*
- *How did you decide how many milk cartons of water it would take to fill a container?*

PREDICTING

Popcorn Predicting

Words You Can Use

kernels, microwave

What You Need

- bag of popcorn kernels
- measuring cup
- plastic cups
- napkins
- popcorn popper
- one tub of water for each small group
- oil for the popcorn popper (unless using an air popper)
- drawing paper
- crayons

What You Do

1. Separate the children into small groups.
2. Pass out one-fourth cup to three-fourths cup of popcorn in a plastic cup to each small group of children.
3. Have the group of children predict how much the partial cups of kernels will pop by filling another plastic cup with water up to where they think the popped corn will fill it.

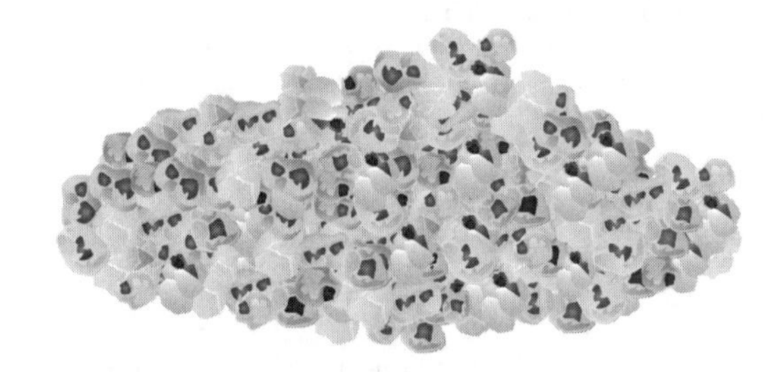

4. Let the children watch you pour their popcorn into the popper and pop it. Let it cool.
5. Now pour the popped corn back into the same cup and have the children compare their predicted levels (the water levels) to the real levels of the popped corn.
6. Encourage the children to share their thoughts.
7. Serve popcorn to the children as a treat!
8. Children can draw pictures of what they remember about the experiment to help them reflect on the process.

Questions You Can Ask

- *Was your prediction right?*
- *Was your prediction too low or too high?*

PREDICTING

Candy Counts

Words You Can Use

piles, sort

What You Need

- variety of candy in multiple colors, either prepackaged mixtures or mixed by you
- one stack of small precut squares of colored paper to match the candy colors for each small group
- napkins
- bags
- chart paper
- chart of color words with matching color pictures

What You Do

1. Separate the children into small groups.
2. Pass out a bag of candy and a napkin to each group. Remind the children not to eat the candy.
3. Pass out a stack of precut colored paper squares to each group.
4. Model for the children how to list the candy colors found in their bags. If they are too young to write, have them pick the colors from the stack of precut paper squares that match the colors of their candy. For example, if you use round, coated chocolate pieces, show them how to match the colors of the coating to the precut paper squares.
5. Next, have the children predict which candy color will appear most often in their bag.
6. Have the children open their bags and count each color of candies. To do this, they can match the candy colors to their colored squares, then count the candy on each square.
7. Ask the children which color appeared the most.
8. Write the results for each color of candy on chart paper. Drawing a bar graph using bar colors that match the candy colors would work well.

Questions You Can Ask

- *Which color of candy appeared the most in your bag?*
- *Was this the color you predicted?*
- *Why do you think there was more of this color than any other?*
- *If you made the candy, which color would you put the most of in each bag? Why?*

Blending Language and Literacy into Science Activities

In the chapter 3 activities you familiarized yourself and the children with the basic science process skills. In chapter 4, you'll find some recipes for the "how" in integrating language and literacy into the science process skills. In actuality, many recipes and combinations of activities support literacy and language integration into science. It is the teacher's skill in understanding the children, their ages and developmental levels, their needs, their ability to attend, and their interests that creates the combination of these activities for each classroom.

It is important that teachers recognize the power of their priority and choices. It is their understanding of young children and how they develop that enables them to create combinations of intentional learning embedded with sensory integration, emotional connections, and play that deepens the learning for the children. It is the skill of the teacher that allows her to select, incorporate, extend, or restrict the activities so that she creates opportunities that internalize learning and set the stage for success for the whole child.

RECIPE FOR MIXING LITERACY INTO SCIENCE ACTIVITIES

In the What You Do section of the chapter 4 activities, you'll find opportunities for enhancing literacy and language activities that are easily and naturally tied into the science activity.

Vocabulary

Words You Can Use, a section that appeared in chapter 3 activities to subtly begin the process of relating science and literacy, is also built into every chapter 4 activity, ensuring that children's vocabularies continue to expand. Teachers are invited to add other appropriate words beyond those listed.

Listening Comprehension

Children may demonstrate their understanding of language and literature by following directions, by responsive and descriptive comments, and by answering open-ended questions or statements. Many opportunities for listening comprehension are built into the recipes. Additional interaction with the suggested books expands the experience and sets up a connection with the activity that builds on the brain's need for connection. The Questions You Can Ask section suggests open-ended questions you can ask the children. The responses may provide additional insight into an individual's listening comprehension.

Verbal Expression

Setting up the activities within a social setting, encouraging comments, asking open-ended questions, and frequently capturing the information in writing encourage verbal expression. The Questions You Can Ask are primarily open-ended questions that are aligned with the Revised Bloom's Taxonomy: Remembering, Understanding, Applying, Analyzing, Evaluating, and Creating.

Sound Play

A Sound Play phonological awareness rhyme, song, fingerplay, or poem is included to launch every activity. Children's ability to hear, understand, and discriminate sounds is of critical importance in preparing to read.

Print and Book Awareness

Teachers are encouraged to use basic book-reading rituals that invite children to identify the author, illustrator, and front and back of the book; track print; connect visual clues; and begin to understand that printed words and speech are related. A detailed description of a Reading Experience book read-aloud is included in the Recipe for Teaching an Integrated Activity section on this page and in Guidelines for the Reading Experience (page 164).

Letter Knowledge and Early Word Recognition

In addition to using the related books, you'll have opportunities for capitalizing on the letter knowledge inherent in the charts, graphs, and children's comments you recorded. Many of the activities have some additional suggestions built in.

Motivation to Read

Using science activities to extend books creates a new and exciting interest in reading.

Written Expression

Every activity presents an opportunity to record comments, words, and data. You may build this into your teaching process, going back to review words and letters and to check for understanding.

RECIPE FOR TEACHING AN INTEGRATED ACTIVITY

Here are some practical suggestions for using the information from the book and integrating a more intentional language and literacy focus into science.

1. Review the items in chapter 2 related to safety and health.
2. Select and review the *Incredible Edible Science* activity.
3. Integrate the language/literacy connections.
   - Select a book from the Reading Experience list. Check the Words You Can Use (vocabulary) and select these words or words from the book as part of your Reading Experience.
   - Provide a Reading Experience for the children (see Guidelines for the Reading Experience, page 164).

- Introduce the Sound Play phonological experience as deemed appropriate. Display the song, tongue-twister, or poem on a chart or sentence strip and post for review, inviting children to read and repeat, and eventually circle words or letters as appropriate. Some children may enjoy using a pointer.
- Make the connection with the science activity with questions such as "Have you ever eaten a pancake?" "What did it taste like?" "Did you put anything on it?" "Have you ever made one yourself?"

4. Conduct the science activity.
    - Prepare all materials and equipment in advance.
    - Review appendix C for objectives relating to competencies in these areas.
    - Reconnect with language and literacy experiences.
    - Add a writing experience when appropriate. You may use the science process skill of prediction and ask children questions such as "What do you think we will need to do first to make our pancakes?" "What ingredients do you think we will need to make a pancake?" or "What do you think will happen if we put the pancake batter on the hot skillet?"
    - Record the children's responses on chart paper in front of the children, once again making the connection between spoken and written language. If appropriate, a child may write a word or letter on the chart paper during the process. You can record the children's predictions and their comments after the experience and use the documentation for comparison and to assist children in making connections.
    - Use every opportunity during the process to encourage verbal expression, including playing around with words.
    - Follow the directions for the activity.
    - Be sure to use this opportunity for assisting children in making social and emotional connections such as communicating with peers, taking responsibility for the selection, monitoring and disposing of their materials, and reviewing the activity.
5. Review the science activity.
    - Review the prediction items with the children either immediately afterward or within a reasonable time limit. Add their comments and reflections on the activity.
    - Integrate the vocabulary and other words. Ask questions and invite comments that help the children reflect on both their independent and group experiences.
    - Use the Questions You Can Ask for ideas in creating open-ended questions.
    - Invite children to draw pictures of their experiences. You may take dictation as a child shares his drawing. Children may also dictate information that you record as they talk about a photo of the science project. These are items that can be used in the children's portfolios.
    - If time allows, circle appropriate words, letters, or vocabulary.
6. Collect information for the child's portfolio.
    - Record anecdotal notes.
    - Review the competencies related to the activity and note the child's abilities and understanding related to these competencies.
    - Make audio or video recordings or photograph the experience to include in your anecdotal files for each child.
    - File any drawing, writing, or dictation that is generated around this activity.

GUIDELINES FOR THE READING EXPERIENCE

The Reading Experience incorporates most of the elements related to integrating language and literacy. Planning and preparing an intentional reading experience for children is crucial in making the most of the activity. Certainly there are many things to consider around the selection of a book—the appropriateness of the book to the age of the children, the number and kinds of illustrations, the quality and, in this instance, its further application to science. In *Incredible Edible Science,* the selection is done for you.

You may also consider exploring the book and setting up the connection to the science activity that can be conducted during center time or at another time during the day so as not to set an unrealistic expectation related to children's ability to attend.

After a book has been selected, the next step is to plan and prepare the read-aloud. To facilitate this process many teachers use a pocket chart (see photo).

The pocket chart contains sentence strips with these items:

- vocabulary words (two to three key words) with pictures
- the name of the book followed by an icon
- the author's name followed by an icon
- the illustrator's name followed by an icon

Prepare in advance three to five open-ended questions for the children. Many teachers choose to simply read a book straight through the first time with minimal discussion, and then doing a second reading during which they ask questions but are also prepared to follow the children's lead in the discussion. Though discussion is important, it is critical that it not be so involved as to derail the young child from grasping the overall concept of the story. This again goes back to your understanding and perception of the young child's ability and behavior during the read-aloud.

It is important that the children be seated comfortably with plenty of room, and positioned in such a way that they can all see the book. Sitting on the floor with the book at the children's eye level is most effective. Doing a read-aloud with a small group gives you more opportunity for individualization and interaction.

It is the comfortable, ritualistic nature of the read-aloud that allows children to gain knowledge and confidence in their abilities to understand the concepts of books and print. Here is a sample dialogue of that ritual:

(The teacher holds up the book and shows it to all the children.)

Teacher: "Let's look at the cover of this book. What do you think this book is about?"

(The teacher provides time for children to ponder and respond. After leading a brief discussion, the teacher tells the children the name of the book. She may decide at this time to introduce vocabulary.)

Teacher: "These are some words we will find in the book."

(The teacher may use the words to further elicit cues. The teacher may also ask some additional questions.)

Teacher: "What does the author do?"

Children: "The author writes the book."

Teacher: "What does the illustrator do?"

Children: "The illustrator draws the pictures."

(The teacher then asks a few more basic questions and the children respond by pointing or gesturing.)

Teacher: "Where is the front of the book? The back of the book? The spine?"

Here are some additional book- and print-related questions you may include as part of the opening ritual later in the year or later in the process:

- Where do we start reading the book?
- Which page do we read first?
- Where do we start reading on the page?
- Can you show me which words we read first? (The teacher and children may use a pointer to demonstrate top to bottom and left to right orientation.)

Again, the amount, the timing, and the use of these questions are all individualized by the teacher with the group. Nevertheless, the repetition of this ritual gives children confidence in understanding how books work and that there is a connection between the spoken and written word.

This literacy enrichment, which is embedded in the chapter 4 activities, purposefully relates to specific science and math skills, particularly the basic science process skills practiced in chapter 3 activities. For more information on which specific skills each activity promotes, see appendix C.

SCIENCE/LITERACY

Good-for-You Food!

Words You Can Use

vegetables, proteins, fruits, grains, dairy, MyPlate, healthy, grow

What You Need

- one or more of the books listed in the Reading Experience section
- magazines, poster board, glue, marker, scissors, MyPlate puzzle pieces, MyPlate poster from www.choosemyplate.gov/multimedia/index.html

What You Do

Use Sound Play to gain children's interest and introduce sounds and words. Explore the vocabulary and topic further by reading one or more of the Reading Experience books. Then use the story to move into the Science Activity.

Sound Play

Sing with the children "If You Are Healthy and You Know It" to the tune of "If You Are Happy and You Know It."

If You Are Healthy and You Know It

If you are healthy and you know it, rub your tummy! Yum! Yum!

If you are healthy and you know it, flex your arm! Strong! Strong!

If you are healthy and you know it, then your strong body will show it!

If you are healthy and you know it, give a cheer! Yea! Yea!

Then sing with them "If You Want to Grow Up Strong" to the tune of "Mary Had a Little Lamb."

If You Want to Grow Up Strong

If you want to grow up strong, grow up strong, grow up strong!

If you want to grow up strong, just eat from MyPlate!

Reading Experience

- *Alligator Arrived with Apples: A Potluck Alphabet Feast* by Crescent Dragonwagon
- *Tommy at the Grocery Store* by Bill Grossman
- *Market!* by Ted Lewin
- *Feast for 10* by Cathryn Falwell
- *Sheep Out to Eat* by Nancy E. Shaw
- *Dinosaurs Alive and Well: A Guide to Good Health* by Laurie Krasny Brown and Marc Brown
- *Nutrition* by Leslie Jean LeMaster

Science Activity

1. Be sure to follow all safety measures (see chapter 2).
2. Introduce the entire MyPlate concept to the children and the part good nutrition plays in healthy development. Then concentrate on only one food group at a time until all groups have been covered.

more →

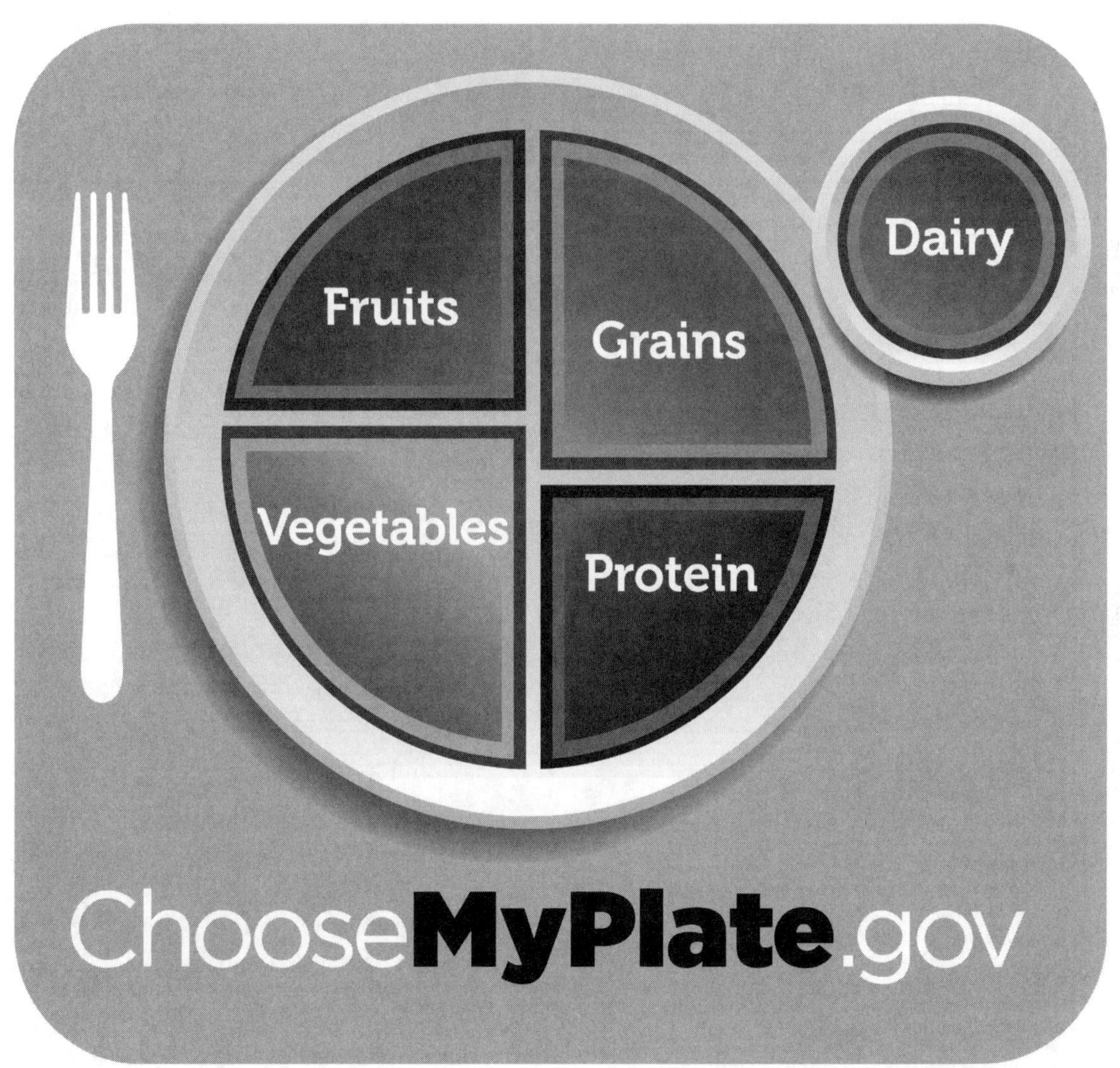

www.choosemyplate.gov/tipsresources/printmaterials.html

more →

3. Copy or enlarge the MyPlate coloring sheet (available at http://www.choosemyplate.gov/downloads/MyPlate/ColoringSheet.pdf) on to poster board.
4. Copy or enlarge the MyPlate icon and make it the same size as the one on your poster board. Cut out the different pieces. These are your puzzle pieces.
5. Make a similar drawing on another sheet of poster board and cut it into sections like a puzzle.
6. As each food group is introduced, have children cut pictures from magazines of the focused food group and glue them on the appropriate puzzle piece. Then use tape to add the puzzle piece to the poster-board model. Be sure children have experience with real objects in a variety of ways. Plastic models are also appropriate.
7. After all the puzzle pieces for the different food groups are completed, review the food groups and put the giant MyPlate puzzle on the floor for the children to put together.

Questions You Can Ask

- *What was our song about? What words or sounds do you remember from the song?*
- *What do you remember about the book we read?*
- *What are the different kinds of food on MyPlate? Why is it important to know about them?*
- *What foods have you tasted in the [name of food group] food group? What were they like?*
- *Which was your favorite? Tell me about the color, texture (inside and out), and taste.*
- *When was the last time that you ate this food? What was it like?*
- *What would happen if we didn't eat foods from all the food groups?*
- *What food would you choose out of each food group to serve to your family and friends?*

More You Can Try

- Use fewer pictures.
- Cut out the pictures in advance and have the children simply select and glue them on the puzzle pieces.
- Have children use plastic models or real objects to group foods on a shower-curtain MyPlate.
- Help children create a book for each food group.
- Have children use a word bank to copy food names into their MyPlate books.
- Invite children to make mobiles illustrating the different food groups on coat hangers.
- Have children use healthy foods to make puppets. Glue foods onto a tongue depressor. Use carrots or celery for the arms and legs, and a tomato or apple for the head. Or use a potato body instead of a tongue depressor. Reinforce the idea that "You are what you eat."
- Have children bring from home pictures or items from the different food groups.
- Read about MyPlate at http://www.choosemyplate.gov.

SCIENCE/LITERACY

It's a Neat Feat to Eat Wheat!

Words You Can Use

cracker, feat, flour, graph, label, puffed, tortilla, wheat

What You Need

- *The Little Red Hen* by Paul Galdone
- puffed-wheat cereal
- whole wheat crackers
- saltine crackers
- pretzels
- whole wheat bread
- flour tortillas
- colored construction paper cut into various shapes, such as a circle, square, rectangle, and triangle, for Sound Play (attribute blocks could also be used)
- small paper plates
- photocopies of a photograph of each child
- chart paper
- product labels, pictures, or samples of each food in baggies
- sticky notes

What You Do

Use Sound Play to gain children's interest and introduce sounds and words. Explore the vocabulary and topic further by reading the Reading Experience book. Then use the story to move into the Science Activity.

Sound Play

Repeat with the children three times:

It's a neat feat to eat wheat!

Repeat with the children three times:

You need a whacker of a cracker to feed that quacker!

Have the children stand in a circle. Give each child a piece of paper cut into a geometric shape, and recite this rhyme:

Acka Backa Soda Cracker

Acka Backa Soda Cracker,
Acka Backa Boo,
Acka Backa Soda Cracker,
Pass to you!

Children march, stamping alternate feet—right, left, right, left—for each word. On "Boo," have them clap their hands. On "you," have the children pass their paper shape to the child on their right. Then say the name of a shape, and have everyone with that shape hold it over their head.

Reading Experience

- *The Little Red Hen* by Paul Galdone

Science Activity

1. Be sure to follow all safety measures (see chapter 2). Be aware of any children who might have an allergy to foods containing gluten.

more →

2. In advance, create a table on chart paper. Set up the chart with six columns—one for each product—and two rows. In the top row, identify each of the six products, puffed wheat cereal, whole wheat crackers, saltine crackers, pretzels, whole wheat bread, and flour tortillas, by attaching labels from product packages (environmental print) or by attaching baggies with samples of the product.
3. Prepare small plates with samples of wheat products to be tasted by the children.
4. Post the chart and have photocopies of each child's picture available with glue.
5. Review *The Little Red Hen* and discuss the wheat that was needed for the bread. (Have oats or grain samples to share with children, if possible.)
6. Introduce each wheat product and taste it.
7. Ask the children which product they like the best. They may choose two if they have difficulty deciding.
8. Review the table.
9. Ask children to predict which items more children will choose as their most favorite and least favorite.
10. Ask children to glue their pictures under the product they like the best. Have them take turns placing their photos on the table starting at the bottom.
11. Look at the completed graph. Invite children to count the photos in each column, and write the totals on sticky notes. Then have children examine the graph to find the most and least favorite.
12. After the children have completed the task, look at the columns that are filled to determine the favorite(s).
13. Provide the favorite(s) in the snack center. Add butter or jam.

Questions You Can Ask

- *What was our rhyme about? What words or sounds do you remember from the rhyme?*
- *What do you remember about* The Little Red Hen?
- *How are the foods we ate alike and different from the bread the Little Red Hen made?*
- *How you can figure out which item goes in which container by the label or box?*

More You Can Try

- Use fewer food items.
- Create a word card for "wheat." Have children look for the word "wheat" on the packaging of the items tasted and items at home. Children may bring items to school to share.
- Have children rank five of the items according to their taste preference.
- Ask the children to re-enact the story *The Little Red Hen*. Provide paper-plate masks or puppets.
- Provide a large container of leftover flour and whole wheat flour, a "squeeze" flour sifter and a "crank" flour sifter, scoop, and measuring cups. Encourage the children to observe the relationship between the sifters and the flour.

SCIENCE/LITERACY

"Just for Me!" Bread

Words You Can Use

electric skillet, flip, individual serving, spatula

What You Need

- *The Little Red Hen* by Paul Galdone
- cornmeal
- all-purpose flour
- baking soda
- salt
- granulated sugar
- buttermilk
- egg whites
- cooking oil
- honey
- small mixing bowl
- large mixing bowl
- measuring cups
- electric or hand mixer
- rubber spatula
- electric skillet
- ladle

What You Do

Use Sound Play to gain children's interest and introduce sounds and words. Explore the vocabulary and topic further by reading the Reading Experience book. Then use the story to move into the Science Activity.

Sound Play

Short'nin' Bread

Put on the skillet, slip on the lid.
Mama's gonna make a little short'nin' bread.
That ain't all
She's gonna do.
Mama's gonna make a little coffee too.

Refrain:
Mama's little baby loves
Short'nin', short'nin',
Mama's little baby loves
Short'nin' bread.
Mama's little baby loves
Short'nin', short'nin',
Mama's little baby loves
Short'nin' bread.

Three little children
Lyin' in bed
Two were sick
And the other 'most dead.
Sent for the doctor
And the doctor said,
"Give those children some short'nin' bread."

(Repeat refrain.)

more →

When those children,
Sick in bed.
Heard that talk
About short'nin' bread,
Popped up well
To dance and sing.
Skipped around and cut
The pigeon wing.

(Repeat refrain.)

Reading Experience

- *The Little Red Hen* by Paul Galdone

Science Activity

1. Be sure to follow all safety measures (see chapter 2).
2. Add ingredients, mix, and cook with groups of five or fewer children.
3. In a small bowl beat stiffly two egg whites and let stand.
4. In a large bowl combine one cup cornmeal, three-quarters cup all-purpose flour, one tablespoon granulated sugar, one teaspoon baking soda, and one-quarter teaspoon salt.
5. Add two cups buttermilk and three table-spoons cooking oil to the cornmeal mixture and beat with electric mixer to combine.
6. Gently fold in beaten egg whites and let stand.
7. Use nonstick spray to coat skillet and then heat the skillet.
8. Help the children ladle one-quarter cup of the batter onto the skillet.
9. Assist children in flipping the cornmeal pancake with the metal spatula.
10. Spray skillet in between use to prevent sticking.
11. Serve the pancakes with honey or syrup.

(Moore, Kerr, and Shulman 1990, 54–55)

Questions You Can Ask

- *What was our song about? What words or sounds do you remember from the song?*
- *What do you remember about* The Little Red Hen?
- *What do you think will happen when we put the mixture into the electric skillet?*
- *Let's mark the cup with a pencil to show where the batter is before we cook it. Then we can check the line after we cook it. What do you think happened?*
- *Does the batter look and taste the same? What do you think happened?*
- *Does this look or taste like the bread you have at home? How is it the same? How is it different?*

More You Can Try

- Use props and act out the song "Short'nin' Bread."

SCIENCE/LITERACY

Hen Pickin's

Words You Can Use

whole, one-half, one-fourth, brush

What You Need

- *The Little Red Hen* by Paul Galdone
- one can refrigerated biscuits
- one-half cup melted margarine
- three-fourths cup granulated sugar mixed with one tablespoon cinnamon
- plastic knife
- cookie sheet
- oven

What You Do

Use Sound Play to gain children's interest and introduce sounds and words. Explore the vocabulary and topic further by reading the Reading Experience book. Then use the story to move into the Science Activity.

Sound Play

Teach this rhyme to the children, repeating it a few times until they can say it with you.

Hickety, Pickety, My Black Hen

Hickety, pickety, my black hen,
She lays eggs for gentlemen.
Gentlemen come every day
To see what my black hen doth lay.
Sometimes nine and sometimes ten,
Hickety, pickety, my black hen.

Reading Experience

- *The Little Red Hen* by Paul Galdone

Science Activity

1. Be sure to follow all safety measures (see chapter 2).
2. In a small group, have children practice making playdough biscuits and cutting them into four even parts—first in half, then in fourths. Demonstrate how to cut the biscuits the same way.
3. When the biscuits are all cut into quarters, dip them into one-half cup of melted margarine and roll in the sugar-cinnamon mixture. Bake at 375 degrees Fahrenheit for four minutes. Makes forty.
4. Eat and enjoy!

more →

Questions You Can Ask

- *What was our rhyme about? What words or sounds do you remember from the rhyme?*
- *What do you remember about the book* The Little Red Hen*?*
- *How many parts did we make out of each biscuit?*
- *How did we do this?*
- *What was your favorite part of the cooking experience?*
- *Was the butter the same or different from butter you have at home?*
- *Is there any other time when it would be helpful to know how to divide items evenly?*

More You Can Try

- Pull bread apart for younger children if you are concerned about them using plastic knives.

SCIENCE/LITERACY

Art Toast

Words You Can Use

dip, food coloring, liquid, toast

What You Need

- *I Spy: An Alphabet in Art* by Lucy Micklethwait
- *Where the Wild Things Are* by Maurice Sendak
- white bread
- toaster
- cotton swab
- food coloring
- milk
- plastic cups for food coloring
- paper towels
- small plates

What You Do

Use Sound Play to gain the children's interest and introduce sounds and words. Explore the vocabulary and topic further by reading one or both of the Reading Experience books. Then use the story to move into the Science Activity.

Sound Play

Use hand motions with the children to make the activity more interesting.

Bread Is Bread, Bread Is Bread!

Roll it
Iron it and
Put it in a press
Toast it
Roast it
Which one tastes best?

Reading Experience

- *I Spy: An Alphabet in Art* by Lucy Micklethwait
- *Where the Wild Things Are* by Maurice Sendak

Science Activity

1. Be sure to follow all safety measures (see chapter 2).
2. Ask children to predict what will happen when the bread is toasted. Record the children's predictions to review later.
3. Mix a small amount of food coloring in one-fourth cup milk. You may use different colors. Use one cotton swab for each color to keep the colors clear.
4. Invite children to dip the cotton swab into the milk and draw a simple picture, face, letter, or design on the toast.
5. Toast bread. The design area will stand out on the toasted bread.
6. As children eat their slices of toast, ask these questions and capture their responses in writing as appropriate.

more →

Questions You Can Ask

- *What was our rhyme about? What words or sounds do you remember from the rhyme?*
- *What do you remember about the two books we read?*
- *How do your predictions compare with your art toast?*
- *What happened to the design on the bread when it was toasted? What did it look like?*
- *What were you thinking about when you created your design?*
- *In your opinion, does putting a design on the bread make it taste better? Worse?*
- *Do you think it makes any difference at all in the taste? (If children are confused, toast a piece of bread without a design and have them taste it.)*

More You Can Try

- Be sure the activity is open-ended, and allow children to create the design of their choice.
- To simplify the activity, use only one color.
- For variety, use other liquids such as orange juice or cola and compare the outcomes.
- Record results by drawing pictures of the results or taking photos.
- Encourage children to write the first letters of their names on the toast.
- Have them draw two faces—one happy, one sad—and compare. Say, "Tell me about a time when your face was happy." "Tell me about a time when your face was sad." "Tell me some other ways your face looks sometimes."
- Connect the activity to the book *Where the Wild Things Are* by Maurice Sendak, by suggesting that children draw a "monster face" on the toast and create "monster toast."

SCIENCE/LITERACY

Roasted Toast

Words You Can Use

candle, cubes, fire, flambé, skewer

What You Need

- *Alligator Arrived with Apples: A Potluck Alphabet Feast* by Crescent Dragonwagon
- uncut loaf of bread
- unscented votive candle
- canning jar
- matches
- bamboo skewers (sharp tips removed)
- bread knife (for teacher only)
- table in outside area
- toaster
- extension cord
- electrical outlet
- napkins
- paper plates

What You Do

Use Sound Play to gain children's interest and introduce sounds and words. Explore the vocabulary and topic further by reading the Reading Experience book. Then use the story to move into the Science Activity.

Sound Play

Repeat this tongue twister from *Alligator Arrived with Apples* with the children three times: *"Bear brought banana bread, biscuits, and butter."*

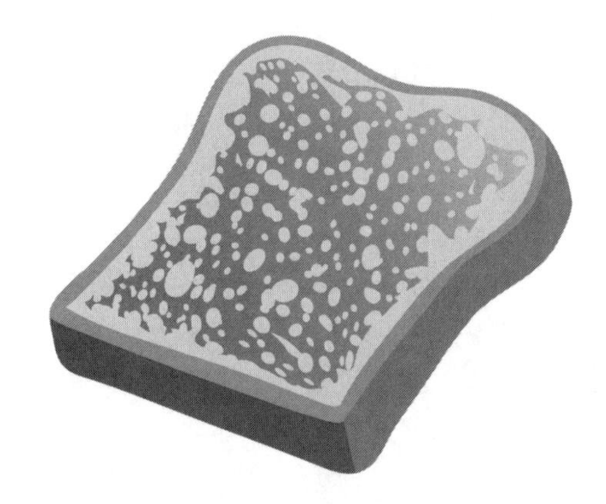

Reading Experience

- *Alligator Arrived with Apples: A Potluck Alphabet Feast* by Crescent Dragonwagon

Science Activity

1. Be sure to follow all safety measures, especially those relating to fire and matches (see chapter 2).
2. Do this activity outside, because any type of flame in a building may set off the fire alarm or extinguishers.
3. Cut a chunk of bread into one-inch cubes and several slices.
4. Place one, two, or three cubes on a bamboo skewer.
5. Place an unscented votive candle in a canning jar.
6. Have children toast the bread over the open candle flame.
7. Toast sliced bread in a toaster, then cut into squares for tasting and comparing.
8. Ask the children questions and capture their responses in writing as appropriate.

more →

Questions You Can Ask

- *What was our tongue twister about? What words or sounds do you remember from the tongue twister?*
- *What do you remember about the book* Alligator Arrived with Apples?
- *What do you think will happen to the bread when you put it over the flame? What about in the toaster?*
- *What happened to the bread when you put it over the flame? What about in the toaster?*
- *In your opinion, does the way we cook the bread change the taste? Can you describe the difference for me?*
- *Which method of cooking is safer? Why?*

More You Can Try

- Roast three bread cubes for each child.
- Have each child examine the bread cubes for consistency of cooking.
- Dip bread into cheese in a fondue pot or cheese warmed in a microwave.

SCIENCE/LITERACY

Roll 'Em Up

Words You Can Use

flatten, rolling pin, topping, waxed paper

What You Need

- *Bread and Jam for Frances* by Russell Hoban
- slices of whole wheat bread
- sandwich toppings of your choice, such as peanut butter, mashed bananas, cream cheese, or jelly
- rolling pin
- waxed paper
- paper towels
- small plates

What You Do

Use Sound Play to gain children's interest and introduce sounds and words. Explore the vocabulary and topic further by reading the Reading Experience book. Then use the story to move into the Science Activity.

Sound Play

Use a rhythm that is similar to "Pat-a-Cake" and incorporate appropriate movements to create a fingerplay for children.

Roll the Bread!

Roll the bread! Roll the bread! Baker girl!
Roll that bread as fast as you can twirl.
Spread it, and roll it, and eat it all up.
Swallow it down with milk in a cup.

Reading Experience

- *Bread and Jam for Frances* by Russell Hoban

Science Activity

1. Be sure to follow all safety measures (see chapter 2). Avoid peanut butter as a sandwich spread if any of the children in your care are allergic to nuts.
2. Place a bread slice on waxed paper.
3. Invite the children to flatten the slice of bread with a rolling pin.
4. Then have the children spread a sandwich topping on the bread, leaving a small border around the edge.
5. The children can roll up the bread, slice it, and eat it! As they eat, ask children the following questions and capture their responses in writing as appropriate.

Questions You Can Ask

- *What do you remember about* Bread and Jam for Frances?
- *What did you do to make the rolled-bread sandwich?*

more →

- *What happened to the bread when you rolled over it with a rolling pin?*
- *In your opinion, did the bread taste the same after it was flattened?*
- *What are some ways you can change the taste of bread?*
- *If you could pick some other toppings, what would you pick?*

More You Can Try

- Use soft flour tortillas instead of bread.
- Use a tortilla press to flatten the bread instead of a rolling pin.
- Use the rolling pin to try to flatten a bagel.
- Use a cookie cutter to cut a shape out of the flattened bread.
- Ask children to bring ideas for toppings they use at home.

SCIENCE/LITERACY

Iron a Sandwich

Words You Can Use

aluminum foil, between, fold, iron, sandwich

What You Need

- *The Giant Jam Sandwich* by John Vernon Lord
- *Bread and Jam for Frances* by Russell Hoban
- bread
- cheese slices
- margarine or butter
- aluminum foil
- an iron
- plastic knives
- paper towels
- small plates

What You Do

Use Sound Play to gain children's interest and introduce sounds and words. Explore the vocabulary and topic further by reading one or both of the Reading Experience books. Then use the story to move into the Science Activity.

Sound Play

Sing to the tune of "Did You Ever See a Lassie?" and incorporate appropriate movements to create a fingerplay for children.

I'm Going to Make a Sandwich!

I'm going to make a sandwich, a sandwich, a sandwich.

I'm going to make a sandwich to eat today.

I'll spread on some mayonnaise,

I might add some mustard.

I'm going to make a sandwich to eat today.

I'm going to make a sandwich to eat today.

I must have some baloney, some cheese,

But not macaroni.

Oh, give me some lettuce,

I'm going to make a sandwich to eat.

Reading Experience

- *The Giant Jam Sandwich* by John Vernon Lord
- *Bread and Jam for Frances* by Russell Hoban

Science Activity

1. Be sure to follow all safety measures (see chapter 2).
2. Place one slice of cheese between two slices of bread.
3. Butter the outside of the bread.
4. Wrap the cheese sandwich in foil.
5. Assist each child in ironing both sides of the sandwich. Set the iron on low, then set the iron on the foil sandwich and leave it for one to two minutes on each side.
6. Let the foil cool for a few seconds.

more →

7. Carefully unwrap the hot foil from the sandwich for each child.
8. With the children, examine the sandwiches for changes.
9. The children can then eat and enjoy!

Questions You Can Ask

- *What was our fingerplay about? What words or sounds do you remember from the fingerplay?*
- *What do you remember about the books we read?*
- *What do you think will happen to the bread when we iron it?*
- *What happened to the bread after it was ironed? What happened to the cheese? Is it the same thing we predicted? Why or why not?*
- *What do you think might happen if you wrapped the sandwich in a paper towel or plastic wrap? Do you think you should eat the sandwich after it is ironed? Why or why not?*

More You Can Try

- Continue exploring the concepts of heat and melting. Make tissue-paper stained glass by placing strips of colored tissue paper between two pieces of waxed paper (waxed sides together) and iron.

SCIENCE/LITERACY

Rice Is Nice, Eat It Twice!

Words You Can Use

cool, ingredients, pudding, stir

What You Need

- *Everybody Cooks Rice* by Norah Dooley and Peter J. Thornton
- three large packages uncooked rice
- two tablespoons cooked rice for each child
- two tablespoons instant pudding for each child
- dry milk for each child
- paper or plastic cups for each child
- one-third cup water for each child
- small measuring cups
- plastic spoons
- paper towels
- rebus recipe for making instant pudding

What You Do

Use Sound Play to gain children's interest and introduce sounds and words. Explore the vocabulary and topic further by reading the Reading Experience book. Then use the story to move into the Science Activity.

Sound Play

Repeat this rhyme with the children three times:

Rice is nice, eat it twice, that's my advice!

Reading Experience

- *Everybody Cooks Rice* by Norah Dooley and Peter J. Thornton

Science Activity

1. Be sure to follow all safety measures (see chapter 2).
2. In advance, cook the rice the children will eat and allow it to cool.
3. Draw the instant pudding rebus recipe and have the ingredients ready in advance.
4. Place three large packages of uncooked rice in a large, open container for exploration. You may provide spoons and small containers for the children to use in pouring and measuring.
5. Demonstrate how to read the rebus recipe as you make the pudding. First measure the instant pudding mix and the dry milk into the cup and stir. Add the water and stir for two minutes while singing "Happy Birthday" four times.
6. Provide each child with a cup for the pudding. Invite children to follow the rebus recipe and make their own pudding.
7. Mark each cup with the child's name. Place all the pudding cups in the refrigerator to cool.
8. When the pudding cups have cooled, the children may add two tablespoons of cooked rice into each one, stir, and eat.

(Johnson and Plemons 1998, 40)

more →

Questions You Can Ask

- *What was our rhyme about? What words or sounds do you remember from the rhyme?*
- *What do you remember about* Everybody Cooks Rice*?*
- *How did you make the pudding? Can you list the ingredients? What did you do first, second, next, last? (Children may use the rebus recipe to retell the experience.)*
- *What did you observe about the pudding while you were stirring and singing "Happy Birthday" four times? Do you think this was important? Why or why not?*

More You Can Try

- Mix different colors of rice in a tube for exploration.
- Use a magnifying glass to examine the rice.
- Prepare brown rice, wild rice, and white rice and have children taste and compare them.

SCIENCE/LITERACY

Chopstick Pick-Up Cakes

Words You Can Use

chopsticks, tongs

What You Need

- *Cleversticks* by Bernard Ashley
- *How My Parents Learned to Eat* by Ina R. Friedman
- small rice cakes
- chopsticks
- small plates
- napkins

What You Do

Use Sound Play to gain children's interest and introduce sounds and words. Explore the vocabulary and topic further by reading one or both of the Reading Experience books. Then use the story to move into the Science Activity.

Sound Play

Repeat this tongue twister with the children:

Cleversticks uses chopsticks.

Cleversticks uses chopsticks.

Cleversticks uses chopsticks.

Reading Experience

- *Cleversticks* by Bernard Ashley
- *How My Parents Learned to Eat* by Ina R. Friedman

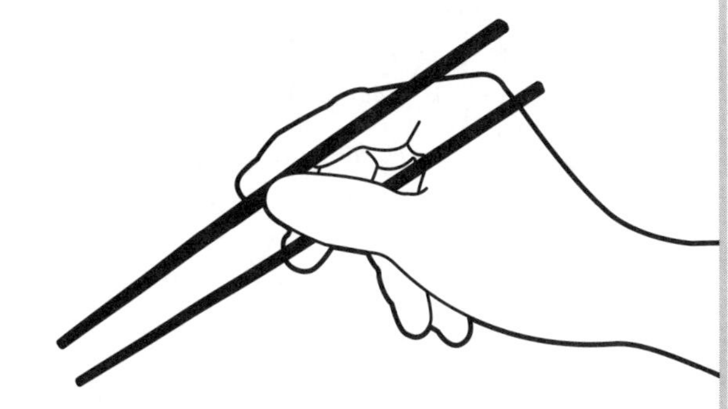

Science Activity

1. Be sure to follow all safety measures (see chapter 2).
2. Demonstrate how to eat with chopsticks. Encourage children to practice holding them or picking up cotton balls with them.
3. Give children some small rice cakes on a plate and encourage them to eat the cakes with their chopsticks.

Questions You Can Ask

- *What was our tongue twister about? What words or sounds do you remember from the tongue twister?*
- *What do you remember about the books we read?*
- *What is the difference between eating with chopsticks and eating with a fork? How are they alike and how are they different?*
- *Which tool is easier to use?*
- *What do you think it might be like if you used a fork to eat the rice cake?*
- *What kinds of suggestions would you give other children who wanted to try chopsticks?*

more →

More You Can Try

- If there are children in the class who use chopsticks at home, have them demonstrate and explain how to use chopsticks to eat.
- Use tongs instead of chopsticks.
- Ice large rice cakes with peanut butter and decorate with raisins, carrot rounds, banana rounds, or orange rounds. Have children identify what is not in the bread group.
- Create faces with food on the rice cakes. Spread with softened cream cheese (any flavor), use canned cheese spread for the mouth, raisins for the eyes, a cherry for the nose, and shredded carrot for the hair.

SCIENCE/LITERACY

Rice Burgers

Words You Can Use

grater, nonstick, skillet

What You Need

- *Everybody Cooks Rice* by Norah Dooley
- rebus recipe for rice burgers
- two tablespoons cooked rice (may use brown or white) for each child
- two teaspoons carrots for each child
- one-half teaspoon chopped parsley for each child
- seasoning (salt, pepper, garlic powder)
- one teaspoon flour for each child
- two teaspoons beaten eggs for each child
- butter or butter spray
- nonstick skillet
- graters in a variety of styles
- spatula
- small plates
- plastic forks
- napkins

What You Do

Use Sound Play to gain children's interest and introduce sounds and words. Explore the vocabulary and topic further by reading the Reading Experience book. Then use the story to move into the Science Activity.

Sound Play

Sing this song with the children to the tune of "Mary Had a Little Lamb."

Everybody Cooks Up Rice

Everybody cooks up rice,
Cooks up rice,
Cooks up rice.
Everybody cooks up rice,
No matter where they live!

Reading Experience

- *Everybody Cooks Rice* by Norah Dooley

Science Activity

1. Be sure to follow all safety measures (see chapter 2), including taking care when using a hot skillet near young children.
2. Prepare the rebus recipe and the ingredients in advance. Cook the rice and chop the parsley.
3. Encourage each child to grate her own carrots. Provide a variety of graters the children may choose to use.
4. Have each child create a rice burger by mixing rice and parsley, adding in the grated carrots, seasoning with a little salt, pepper, and/or garlic, and mixing in flour and beaten eggs. Before and after they pat the mixture into a burger, be sure children wash their hands thoroughly.
5. Fry the burgers in a buttered pan, flipping them midway. Serve a few children at a time.

more →

Questions You Can Ask

- *What was our song about? What words or sounds do you remember from the song?*
- *What do you remember about* Everybody Cooks Rice?
- *What ingredients did you use to make the rice burger?*
- *If you wanted to make a hamburger, would you use the same ingredients?*
- *How are a hamburger and a rice burger different? How are they the same?*
- *Which burger do you like best and why?*
- *How do you flip a burger?*
- *What happens if the burger sticks to the pan? What do you do?*
- *Do you think you will make rice burgers again?*

More You Can Try

- Try additional rice recipes found in *Everybody Cooks Rice.*
- Have children bring rice recipes from home and make a class cookbook.

SCIENCE/LITERACY

Yummy, Messy Rice!

Words You Can Use

glimmering, glittery, messy

What You Need

- *How My Parents Learned to Eat* by Ina R. Friedman
- two cups cooked rice
- two beaten eggs
- two cups of any of the following: green peas, chopped carrots, bean sprouts, celery, water chestnuts, broccoli, snow peas, mushrooms
- soy sauce
- electric skillet or wok
- cooking oil
- spatula or chopsticks
- paper towels
- small bowls
- chopsticks for each child

What You Do

Use Sound Play to gain children's interest and introduce sounds and words. Explore the vocabulary and topic further by reading the Reading Experience book. Then use the story to move into the Science Activity.

Sound Play

Read the entire poem. Invite children to repeat each line three times, one line at a time.

Gobbling Rice

Glimmering, glittery, glistening rice,
Gracious, golden, gourmet taste.
Grazing, gobbling, giggling, and nice,
Grinning, gulping, gusto, no waste.

Reading Experience

- *How My Parents Learned to Eat* by Ina R. Friedman

Science Activity

1. Be sure to follow all safety measures (see chapter 2).
2. Cook the rice in advance and allow it to cool.
3. Place some raw vegetables in small bowls and label each bowl. Set aside enough vegetables to be cooked.
4. Invite the children to examine and taste the raw vegetables.
5. Cook the (untouched) raw vegetables you set aside over low heat in oil until done, stirring occasionally.
6. Move vegetables to one side of the pan and scramble the eggs in the same pan.
7. Add cooked rice and soy sauce. Mix and heat.
8. Serve the yummy, messy stir-fried rice to the children with chopsticks and offer additional soy sauce.
9. Ask children questions about the cooking experience and capture their responses in writing as appropriate.

more →

Questions You Can Ask

- *What was our poem about? What words or sounds do you remember from the poem?*
- *What do you remember about* How My Parents Learned to Eat?
- *How do you make "Yummy, Messy Rice"? What did you do first, second, last?*
- *What happened to the vegetables when you cooked them in the skillet? What did they look like? Were they the same or different after they were cooked?*
- *What happened when you used the chopsticks to eat the rice?*
- *Do you think there was anything we could have done to the food to make it easier to eat with chopsticks? What might that have been?*

More You Can Try

- If there are children in the class who use chopsticks at home, have them demonstrate and explain how to use chopsticks to eat.
- Create a class book with children's descriptions and illustrations of how they learned to eat.
- Create a photo story of the activity. Invite children to put the story in order—what happened first, second, and so forth—and retell the story of the activity.

SCIENCE/LITERACY

Gobble and Giggle Necklace

Words You Can Use

necklace, nibble, patterning, sorting, gobble, giggle

What You Need

- *ABC, I Like Me!* by Nancy Carlson
- index cards
- package labels from the food items used
- one large bag of shoestring licorice or yarn
- food items for stringing, such as small pretzels or breakfast cereals with holes
- waxed paper
- unifix cubes or pattern cards

What You Do

Use Sound Play to gain children's interest and introduce sounds and words. Explore the vocabulary and topic further by reading the Reading Experience book. Then use the story to move into the Science Activity.

Sound Play

Yummy, Yummy, Take a Bite

Yummy, yummy, take a bite.

One, two, I can touch my shoe. (Child eats two items off the necklace and touches the top of his shoe.)

Yummy, yummy, take a bite.

Three, four, I want MORE! (Child eats two more items off the necklace and rubs her tummy.)

Yummy, yummy, take a bite.

Five, six, I can do a trick! (Child eats two more items off the necklace and twirls around or does a trick of his choice.)

Yummy, yummy, take a bite.

How many are left?

One, two, three, four . . . (Child counts the items that are left.)

Note: After the children have completed the Science Activity, return to this rhyme and have children do the actions in parentheses.

Reading Experience

- *ABC, I Like Me!* by Nancy Carlson

Science Activity

1. Be sure to follow all safety measures (see chapter 2).
2. In advance, glue package labels from the items you are using onto index cards and create environmental-print cards.
3. Place food items in bowls and label with index cards.
4. Give each child a piece of waxed paper.
5. Create a pile of food items and let children sort and explore them, including tasting (approximately one or two of each item for exploration).
6. Demonstrate different patterns for children using food items, unifix cubes, or pattern cards, depending on the developmental stage of the children. Align the level of pattern with the child's ability to successfully replicate it.

more →

7. Let children choose items to use for patterning, practicing first on the waxed paper.
8. Check patterns and note child's progress.
9. Cut licorice strings or yarn in twenty-four-inch lengths. Tie a knot on one end of the licorice string or yarn and have children string their patterns.
10. Limit the number of items on licorice from ten to twenty-five, depending on children's ability to pattern and count. Be aware of setting limitations so that children avoid sugar highs.
11. Tie ends of necklaces together.
12. Repeat the Sound Play with the actions in parentheses.

Questions You Can Ask

- *What was our poem about? What words or sounds do you remember from the poem?*
- *What do you remember about the book* ABC, I Like Me!
- *How did you make your pattern? Describe the items you chose and the type of pattern you created.*
- *How did you keep the pattern in order and then repeat it over and over?*
- *Why did you decide to do your pattern this way?*
- *If you made another necklace, what materials would you choose? Why?*
- *Do you see any other patterns like yours on someone else's necklace or in our room?*

More You Can Try

- Limit pattern choices.
- Have children create matching patterns using pattern cards of increasing difficulty.
- Have children make patterns with different materials.

SCIENCE/LITERACY

Catch Me If You Can!

Words You Can Use

catch, compare, describe, ginger, hide, hiding place, run, tell

What You Need

- one or more books listed in the Reading Experience section
- two boxes of gingerbread mix
- water
- shortening
- raisins
- mixing bowl
- measuring cup
- wooden spoon
- waxed paper
- cookie sheet
- one gingerbread boy cookie cutter for each group of children
- small plates
- hot pad
- paper towels

What You Do

Use Sound Play to gain children's interest and introduce sounds and words. Explore the vocabulary and topic further by reading one or more of the Reading Experience books. Then use the story to move into the Science Activity.

Sound Play

Use a gingerbread boy/girl puppet to help you engage children in the activity as you say this poem with them:

I Can Catch You!

I'm the gingerbread boy, you can't catch me! You can't catch me!

I'm the kid, I can catch you! I can catch you!

Gotcha!

Lickity lips, lickity lips, lickity lips.

Gobble, Gobble, Gobble!

Yum, Yum!

Reading Experience

- *The Gingerbread Boy* by Richard Egielski
- *You Can't Catch Me* by Charlotte Doyle
- *The Runaway Tortilla* by Eric A. Kimmel
- *The Gingerbread Girl* by Lisa Campbell Ernst

Science Activity

1. Be sure to follow all safety measures (see chapter 2).
2. Practice making a gingerbread boy with playdough and a cookie cutter.
3. Separate children into small groups, and let them assist you in mixing up the ingredients. Invite them to smell the ingredients. Talk about ginger spice.
4. Give each group some dough and have them cut out a gingerbread boy cookie and use raisins for the eyes.
5. Bake the cookies and allow them to cool.

more →

Questions You Can Ask

- *What was our poem about? What words or sounds do you remember from the poem?*
- *What do you remember about the book(s) we read?*
- *How did you make the gingerbread boy? What did you do first, second, next, last?*
- *Tell me where you would hide if you were the gingerbread boy.*
- *Tell me why the gingerbread boy wants to hide. What will happen if he doesn't try to run away?*
- *What do you think we should do with our gingerbread boys?*

More You Can Try

- Compare and contrast *The Gingerbread Boy* and *The Runaway Tortilla*.
- Make gingerbread boys and tortillas with playdough. Bring in real tortillas and gingerbread-boy cookies to taste.
- Demonstrate how to flatten the playdough with a rolling pin and then a tortilla press.
- Read *The Gingerbread Boy* first. Introduce *The Runaway Tortilla*. Have children predict what might be the same and different in the two books.
- Compare *The Runaway Tortilla* with *The Gingerbread Boy* How are they the same? How are they different? Write their responses as the children share them.
- Make a bar graph. Have children vote on which story they like best and graph their results.
- Create your own story about runaway food.
- Hide paper versions of the gingerbread boy and the runaway tortilla around the room, and give the children simple clues to help them find them.
- Have the children use stencils to trace gingerbread boys, then cut them out. Give them white paint and cotton swabs to decorate their cutouts.

SCIENCE/LITERACY

Taco Food Bar

Words You Can Use

assembly line, taco, salsa; ordering words—first, second, third, fourth, last, middle

What You Need

- *Let's Make Tacos* by Mary Hill
- one taco shell for each child
- one can refried beans and/or one pound ground beef cooked in advance with one package of taco seasoning
- one pound chunk cheddar cheese
- one head of lettuce
- sour cream
- one can sliced black olives
- mild salsa
- waxed paper
- cheese grater
- plastic knives
- can opener
- paper towels
- napkins
- small plates

What You Do

Use Sound Play to gain children's interest and introduce sounds and words. Explore the vocabulary and topic further by reading the Reading Experience book. Then use the story to move into the Science Activity.

Sound Play

Repeat this tongue twister with the children three times:

Tasty taco in my tummy totally yummy!

Reading Experience

- *Let's Make Tacos* by Mary Hill

Science Activity

1. Be sure to follow all safety measures (see chapter 2).
2. Invite children to grate cheese and shred lettuce onto waxed paper. Use different kinds of graters.
3. Place additional ingredients on plates and label them.
4. Arrange an assembly line in this order: taco shell, beans/meat, lettuce, cheese, sour cream, olives, salsa.
5. Explain how an assembly line works by demonstrating how to make a taco, beginning with the shell and adding more ingredients at each station.

more →

6. Encourage the children to move through the line and prepare their own tacos.
7. Eat the tacos!

Questions You Can Ask

- *What was our tongue twister about? What words or sounds do you remember from the tongue twister?*
- *What do you remember about* Let's Make Tacos*?*
- *How did you make your taco? What did you do first, second, next, last?*
- *How did the food feel when you touched it with your tongue and put it into your mouth?*
- *Did you notice anything crunchy? Anything smooth? What were those things?*
- *Have you ever made anything using an assembly line before? What do you think was good about doing it this way? Was there anything you would do differently?*
- *What other ingredients might you like to add to your taco?*

More You Can Try

- Compare soft flour tortillas with crunchy tortillas made from corn. How are they the same? How are they different?

SCIENCE/LITERACY

Popcorn Sculpture

Words You Can Use

flavored gelatin, microwave-safe, oven mitts, sculpt

What You Need

- *Norman the Doorman* by Don Freeman
- two cups popped popcorn
- bag of mini-marshmallows
- three packages flavored gelatin (different flavors and colors)
- one-fourth cup margarine plus one tablespoon
- optional foods for decoration, such as bean sprouts, celery sticks or carrot sticks
- microwave oven
- oven mitts
- waxed paper
- three bowls
- large microwave-safe bowl
- large wooden spoon

What You Do

Use Sound Play to gain children's interest and introduce sounds and words. Explore the vocabulary and topic further by reading the Reading Experience book. Then use the story to move into the Science Activity.

Sound Play

I'm a Little Popcorn

Still and quiet, still and quiet. (Child squats quietly on floor.)

I feel hot. I feel hotter. (Child wipes sweat off brow.)

I am going to explode! (Child starts shaking.)

Pop! (Child jumps up.)

Reading Experience

- *Norman the Doorman* by Don Freeman

Science Activity

1. Be sure to follow all safety measures (see chapter 2).

Note: An adult must prepare the marshmallow-popcorn mixture and be ready to cool and serve it to children immediately for the activity.

2. Place the margarine and the marshmallows in the microwave and heat until marshmallows are puffed, about one and one-half to two minutes. Remove the bowl from the microwave and stir the mixture with a wooden spoon.
3. Divide the popped popcorn into three bowls. Add a different flavor of gelatin powder to each bowl.
4. Pour one-third of the melted marshmallow mixture into each of the three bowls and mix each bowl until the gelatin colors the marshmallow and the popcorn is evenly covered.

more →

5. Place bowls of colored popcorn on table.
6. Have children work in small groups. Provide a waxed-paper surface for each child to work on.
7. Be sure to cool down the mixture enough that it can be handled safely but not so much that the marshmallow hardens.
8. Have the children rub some margarine on their hands to prevent the marshmallow from sticking to their fingers.
9. Invite the children to choose one or more colors/flavors of popcorn mixture and to create sculptures. They may use the optional foods for decoration before they eat their creations.

Questions You Can Ask

- *What was our poem about? What words or sounds do you remember from the poem?*
- *What do you remember about* Norman the Doorman?
- *Tell me what might have happened if we had worked with the popcorn mixture before it cooled down.*
- *Tell me about your experience sculpting popcorn. Did the popcorn mix do what you wanted it to? How did you decide to handle the situation?*
- *Describe to me what happens to the popcorn mixture as it cools.*

More You Can Try

- Before the activity, put a king-sized sheet on the floor. Place an air popper in the middle of the sheet and discuss safety concerns.
- Carefully seat children around the edge of the sheet and supervise those children who might not be able to maintain their safe position.
- Pop the corn and help children observe what happens.
- Substitute marshmallow cream for marshmallows if you wish. Be sure and coat children's hands with a cooking spray or spray butter to minimize sticking during the sculpture process. Let sculptures dry and then eat them.

SCIENCE/LITERACY

Alphabet Pretzels

Words You Can Use

dissolve, dough, knead, yeast

What You Need

- *Walter the Baker* by Eric Carle
- *My Daddy Is a Pretzel: Yoga for Parents and Kids* by Baron Baptiste and Sophie Fatus
- *The First Football ABC Pretzel Book* by Beti Kristof
- package of yeast
- warm water
- honey
- salt
- flour
- measuring spoons
- measuring cups
- small bowls or cups for mixing ingredients (one for each pair of children)
- waxed paper
- cookie sheet
- coarse salt
- one egg, beaten
- oven
- paper goods

What You Do

Use Sound Play to gain children's interest and introduce sounds and words. Explore the vocabulary and topic further by reading one or more of the Reading Experience books. Then use the story to move into the Science Activity.

Sound Play

Twist and Learn

Twist, stretch, form, and turn.
Making the alphabet is how I learn.

I can make "A." (hands overhead, palms together)
I can make "C." (lay on ground and curl toward left)
I can make "O." (lay on ground and make a circle with your body)
I can make "E." (draw on paper)

Twist, stretch, form, and turn.
Eating the alphabet is how I learn.

Reading Experience

- *Walter the Baker* by Eric Carle
- *My Daddy Is a Pretzel: Yoga for Parents and Kids* by Baron Baptiste and Sophie Fatus
- *The First Football ABC Pretzel Book* by Beti Kristof

Science Activity

1. Be sure to follow all safety measures (see chapter 2).
2. Have children work in pairs to mix ingredients and form letters.
3. Provide each pair with a cup or small bowl to mix their ingredients.

more →

4. Have each pair of children dissolve one tablespoon of yeast into one-half cup of warm water.
5. Next they can add one teaspoon of salt and one teaspoon of honey to the yeast water.
6. Then they will add one and one-third cup flour and mix it in to form a dough.
7. Divide the dough in half and give each child one half. Show the children how to knead the dough on waxed paper.
8. Demonstrate and help the children roll the dough into "snakes" and form letters.
9. When children have finished forming letters, remind them to wash their hands thoroughly.
10. Brush their letters with beaten egg and sprinkle with coarse salt. Bake the pretzel letters for ten minutes at 425 degrees Fahrenheit. Let them cool before allowing the children to eat them.

Questions You Can Ask

- *What was our poem about? What words or sounds do you remember from the poem?*
- *What do you remember about the book(s) we read?*
- *How did you make your pretzel letter? What did you do first, second, third, fourth, next, and last?*
- *Show me how you used your hands to knead. Why do you think this was important?*
- *What letters did you make? How did you figure out how to make them with the pretzel dough? Show me the letters that are in your name. Show me some curved lines, straight lines, and lines that are both curved and straight.*
- *What letters did your tongue beg you to eat first?*

More You Can Try

- Use playdough or clay.
- Use canned biscuits instead of yeast dough.
- Have the children form all the letters of their names.
- To simplify, draw a single letter on a piece of paper. Lay it under waxed paper. Let the child form the dough on top of the letter, using the letter as a model.

SCIENCE/LITERACY

Eating The Three Bears

Words You Use

big, bigger, biggest, large, medium, small

What You Need

- *The Three Bears* by Paul Galdone
- *Brown Bear, Brown Bear, What Do You See?* by Bill Martin Jr.
- one bagel for each child
- one vanilla wafer for each child
- two miniature crackers for each child
- peanut butter
- chocolate chips
- round-shaped breakfast cereal with holes in the center (enough for each child to have several pieces)
- waxed paper
- small paper plates
- plastic knives
- small containers

What You Do

Use Sound Play to gain children's interest and introduce sounds and words. Explore the vocabulary and topic further by reading one or both of the Reading Experience books. Then use the story to move into the Science Activity.

Sound Play

Bears Eat Honey

Bears eat honey.
Cows eat corn.
What do you eat
When you get up in the morn?
Monkeys eat bananas.
Cows eat corn.
What do you eat
When you get up in the morn?
Baby eats oatmeal.
Cows eat corn.
What do you eat
When you get up in the morn?

Reading Experience

- *The Three Bears* by Paul Galdone
- *Brown Bear, Brown Bear, What Do You See?* by Bill Martin Jr.

Science Activity

1. Be sure to follow all safety measures (see chapter 2).
2. Compare the bagels, vanilla wafers, and crackers using the words "large," "medium," and "small." Discuss how these same words could describe The Three Bears: Papa Bear, Mama Bear, and Baby Bear.
3. Have children decorate the food items to resemble The Three Bears. Demonstrate how to make The Three Bears.

more →

4. For Papa Bear, spread peanut butter on a bagel half, place a cracker over the bagel hole, and place crackers as ears. Use the chocolate chips as the eyes and nose, using peanut butter as glue.
5. For Mama Bear, spread peanut butter on a vanilla wafer and decorate it in a similar fashion to the Papa Bear snack.
6. For Baby Bear, spread peanut butter on a cracker. Use round cereal pieces for the ears and mouth, and chocolate chips for the eyes and nose.
7. Variations: use chocolate sprinkles or coconut for fur; use other cereals, nuts, and raisins for features.
8. Compare and eat!

Questions You Can Ask

- *What was our rhyme about? What words or sounds do you remember from the rhyme?*
- *What do you remember about the book(s) we read?*
- *How did you create Papa Bear, Mama Bear, and Baby Bear with your bagels, wafers, and crackers? What were the steps?*
- *How are these pretend bears like the Papa Bear, Mama Bear, and Baby Bear in the story? How are they different?*
- *Do you have three-bear sizes in your family? Tell me about your family. What sizes are the people in your family?*
- *How do you think we could make Goldilocks?*
- *If we made Goldilocks, what do you think she might say to The Three Bears? What would they say to her?*

More You Can Try

- Retell *The Three Bears* using the food bears.
- Take photos of The Three Bears food items and have children retell the story and create an individual book or dictation page relating to the story.
- Have children create an extension to the story of The Three Bears by asking them such questions as "Did Goldilocks come back and apologize?" and "Did Mama Bear call Goldilocks's mother?"

SCIENCE/LITERACY

Bagel Exploration

Words You Can Use

bagel, balance scale, flavor, float, magnifying glass, sink

What You Need

- *Where on Earth Is My Bagel?* by Frances Park and Ginger Park
- one bagel for each child
- one magnifying glass for each child
- paper plates
- large tub
- water
- paper towels

What You Do

Use Sound Play to gain children's interest and introduce sounds and words. Explore the vocabulary and topic further by reading the Reading Experience book. Then use the story to move into the Science Activity.

Sound Play

Sing this song with the children to the tune of "Turkey in the Straw."

The Bagel Song

Oh, I ran around the corner,
And I ran around the block.
I ran right into the baker shop.
I grabbed me a bagel,
And I grabbed it with ease,
And I handed the lady,
A five-cent piece.
She looked at the nickel,
And she looked at me.
She said, "This nickel,
Ain't no good to me."
There's a hole in the nickel,
And it goes right through."
Said I, "There's a hole in your bagel, too!
Thanks for the bagel. Good-bye!"
(Adapted from "The Donut Song" © 2004 by Pam Schiller.)

Reading Experience

- *Where on Earth Is My Bagel?* by Frances Park and Ginger Park

Science Activity

1. Be sure to follow all safety measures (see chapter 2).
2. Bring in a variety of flavored bagels.
3. Pass out one bagel and a paper plate to each child.
4. Give each child a magnifying glass and invite the children observe their bagels on their plates.
5. Have the children draw pictures of their bagels.

more →

6. Put one bagel in water for about thirty minutes.
7. After thirty minutes, remove the bagel.
8. Ask the children to draw pictures of the soaked bagel.

Questions You Can Ask

- *What was our song about? What words or sounds do you remember from the song?*
- *What do you remember about* Where on Earth Is My Bagel?
- *Tell me what your bagel looks like. How is it unique?*
- *What happened when the bagel was put in water? Why do you think that happened?*

More You Can Try

- Separate the children into small groups. Give each group a bag of bagels. Have the children sort/classify their bagels into piles by a common attribute. Have the children then report on what attributes they used to classify their bag of bagels.
- Give each small group of children a bag of bagels of different sizes. Have the children order the bagels in their bag from smallest to largest. Have the children draw pictures of what they did in this activity.
- Give each small group of children a balance scale and bagels in a variety of sizes. Have the children place a bagel on one side of the scale and another bagel on the other side. Have them decide which one weighs the most.

SCIENCE/LITERACY

The Three Bears' Porridge

Words You Can Use

cold, divide, hot, predict

What You Need

- one or more books listed in the Reading Experience below
- individual packets of instant oatmeal and instant Cream of Wheat
- brown sugar
- raisins
- finely chopped apples
- warm water
- small pitcher
- individual foam cups or bowls
- plastic spoons
- paper towels

What You Do

Use Sound Play to gain children's interest and introduce sounds and words. Explore the vocabulary and topic further by reading one or more of the Reading Experience books. Then use the story to move into the Science Activity.

Sound Play

Peas Porridge Hot

Peas porridge hot.
Peas porridge cold.
Peas porridge in the pot
Nine days old.
Some like it hot.
Some like it cold.
Some like it in the pot
Nine days old!

Porridge Is Bubbling

Porridge is bubbling, bubbling hot.
Stir it round and round in the pot.
The bubbles plip.
The bubbles plop.
It's ready to eat all bubbling hot.
Wake up, baby.
Wake up soon.
We'll eat the porridge with a spoon.

Reading Experience

- *The Three Bears* by Paul Galdone
- *Somebody and the Three Blairs* by Marilyn Tolhurst and Simone Abel
- *Deep in the Forest* by Brinton Turkle

Science Activity

1. Be sure to follow all safety measures (see chapter 2).
2. Explain that porridge is like oatmeal or Cream of Wheat. Ask children to share their experiences with these foods.
3. Have children work with a partner. Divide a packet of oatmeal into two cups and divide a packet of Cream of Wheat into two cups for each pair of children. Each child should receive two cups, one of each mixture.

more →

4. Have children stir the dry mixtures as they add warm water, one tablespoon at a time, until the mixtures are the proper consistency.
5. Have children taste the unsweetened mixtures. Then invite them to add one teaspoon of brown sugar, two or three raisins, and/or a teaspoon of finely chopped apples. **Note**: Some children may have to taste these ingredients in advance to be sure they want to add them.
6. Ask the children to compare, eat, and enjoy!

Questions You Can Ask

- *What was our rhyme about? What words or sounds do you remember from the rhyme?*
- *What do you remember about the book(s) we read?*
- *How did you make your porridge? What else could you put in the porridge?*
- *Have children predict which porridge they might like best—oatmeal or Cream of Wheat. Record their predictions on a piece of chart paper.*
- *When the activity is completed, ask children to share which porridge they liked best. Add their responses to the chart paper. Compare their answers with their predictions. How many liked oatmeal? How many liked Cream of Wheat?*
- *How did adding raisins, brown sugar, or apples change the flavor of the porridge?*

More You Can Try

- Prepare the oatmeal and cream of wheat in advance.
- Provide the children with spoons, cups, sand, and water in the unstructured materials center and pretend to make more porridge.

SCIENCE/LITERACY

Measure with Spaghetti

Words You Can Use

different, longer, same, shorter

What You Need

- *Daddy Makes the Best Spaghetti* by Anna Grossnickle Hines
- *Cloudy with a Chance of Meatballs* by Judi Barrett
- long unbroken lengths of uncooked spaghetti
- classroom items that are longer or shorter than a length of spaghetti

What You Do

Use Sound Play to gain children's interest and introduce sounds and words. Explore the vocabulary and topic further by reading one or both of the Reading Experience books. Then use the story to move into the Science Activity.

Sound Play

Have children use motions and words at the end of each phrase.

My Daddy and I Cook in the Kitchen

My daddy and I cook in the kitchen.
I like the way he laughs.
He uses every pot and pan,
I think just because he can.
Bang, Bang, Bang. (Act as if wooden spoon is hitting a pot.)

My daddy and I cook in the kitchen.
I like the way it smells.
He stirs in this and that.
Did I see him stir in the cat?
Meow, Meow, Meow!

My daddy and I cook in the kitchen.
I like the way he lets me help.
Sometimes I get to lick the icing bowl
And drink a glass of chocolate milk that's cold.
Slurp, slurp, slurp. (Act as if you are slurping the milk through a straw.)

My daddy and I cook in the kitchen.
I like the way he laughs.
It makes me yummy and warm in a way
That makes it the best part of the day!
Sigh, Sigh, Sigh. (Hug yourself and sigh with happiness.)

Reading Experience

- *Daddy Makes the Best Spaghetti* by Anna Grossnickle Hines
- *Cloudy with a Chance of Meatballs* by Judi Barrett

Science Activity

1. Be sure to follow all safety measures (see chapter 2).
2. Have children explore spaghetti. As they explore, don't worry if some pieces break.

more →

3. Have children compare spaghetti to items in the classroom to determine whether they are longer, shorter, or the same.
4. Invite children to look for items that are the same as two or three lengths of spaghetti.
5. Have children predict how many lengths of spaghetti certain items are and then check their predictions.

Questions You Can Ask

- *What was our song about? What words or sounds do you remember from the song?*
- *What do you remember about the book(s) we read?*
- *How did you measure with the spaghetti to keep it from getting broken?*
- *What items are longer than your spaghetti? Shorter? The same?*
- *Where is something in the classroom that is "two spaghettis" long?*

More You Can Try

- Cook, rinse, and cool spaghetti.
- Invite children to create designs with spaghetti on colored paper. Let the spaghetti dry on the paper.

SCIENCE/LITERACY

Pancakes and Flapjacks

Words You Can Use

fat, flat, flip, toss

What You Need

- *Marsupial Sue Presents the Runaway Pancake* (book and CD) by John Lithgow and Jack E. Davis
- *If You Give a Pig a Pancake* by Laura Numeroff
- one teaspoon beaten egg
- two tablespoons prepared baking mix
- two tablespoons milk
- oil or cooking spray
- one cup strawberries and one-fourth cup unsweetened frozen apple-juice concentrate
- five-ounce paper cups or small bowls
- measuring spoons
- plastic spoons
- plastic knives
- electric skillet
- spatula (pancake turner)
- blender
- paper towels
- small plates
- napkins

What You Do

Use Sound Play to gain children's interest and introduce sounds and words. Explore the vocabulary and topic further by reading one or both of the Reading Experience books. Then use the story to move into the Science Activity.

Sound Play

Make a Pancake

Make a pancake pat, pat, pat.
Do not make it fat, fat, fat.
You must make it flat, flat, flat.
Make a pancake just like that.
(© 2003 by Pam Schiller)

Reading Experience

- *Marsupial Sue Presents the Runaway Pancake* (book and CD) by John Lithgow and Jack E. Davis
- *If You Give a Pig a Pancake* by Laura Numeroff

Science Activity

Note: Group size depends on age and teacher experience. Two to four children at a time is average.

1. Be sure to follow all safety measures (see chapter 2).
2. Make pink syrup in advance by combining one cup strawberries with one-fourth cup unsweetened frozen apple-juice concentrate. Process in a blender.

more →

3. Beat egg in advance.
4. Have children measure the prepared baking mix, milk, and egg into a paper cup or small bowl and mix it with a spoon:
   - two tablespoons prepared baking mix
   - two tablespoons milk (adjust liquid to baking mix until you achieve the right consistency for batter)
   - one teaspoon beaten egg
5. Apply oil or cooking spray to the skillet.
6. Have each child carefully pour the mixture into the skillet to form a pancake.
7. Point out how to tell when the pancakes are ready to be flipped (when bubbles start to form). Demonstrate how to flip a pancake with a spatula, then allow each child to flip a pancake.
8. Enjoy the pancakes with pink syrup!

Questions You Can Ask

- *What was our rhyme about? What words or sounds do you remember from the rhyme?*
- *What do you remember about the book(s) we read?*
- *What happens to the pancake that tells you it is time to turn it over?*
- *Show me how you flipped it over. What were you thinking about while you were doing this?*
- *What other pancake shapes could you make?*

More You Can Try

- Cut four-inch "pancakes" out of brown cardboard and let the children practice flipping the pancakes during dramatic play.
- Have children balance a cardboard pancake on a pancake turner and walk across the room and back without dropping it.
- Mark cardboard pancakes with matching numbers or colors. Use a pancake turner to flip over the pancakes to find the matching pairs.
- Have children hold an aluminum pie pan containing a cardboard pancake with both hands. Have children toss the pancake in the air and try to catch it.

SCIENCE/LITERACY

Bunny Foo-Foo

Words You Can Use

construct, part, whole

What You Need

- one or more of the books listed in the Reading Experience below
- one whole pear
- canned pear halves
- maraschino cherry halves
- blanched almonds
- raisins
- cottage cheese
- celery sticks
- iceberg lettuce
- carrot sticks
- plastic spoons
- bowls
- plates
- can opener

What You Do

Use Sound Play to gain children's interest and introduce sounds and words. Explore the vocabulary and topic further by reading one or more of the Reading Experience books. Then use the story to move into the Science Activity.

Sound Play

Here Is a Bunny

Here is a bunny with ears so funny, (Bend two fingers over thumb.)

And here is a hole in the ground. (Make a hole with left hand.)

When a noise he hears, he pricks up his ears, (Hold ears straight.)

And hops into his hole so round. (Hop bunny over into the hole.)

Reading Experience

- *Little Rabbit Foo Foo* by Michael Rosen and Arthur Robins
- *A Bedtime Story* by Mem Fox
- *Guess How Much I Love You* by Sam McBratney

Science Activity

1. Be sure to follow all safety measures (see chapter 2).
2. Wash the pear and lettuce in advance. Place other ingredients in bowls and label them.
3. Introduce the children to the ingredients. Start with the whole pear. Encourage the children to examine and describe it. Cut the pear in half to reveal the seeds. Taste the pear. Examine the canned pears and compare them to the fresh pear.

more →

4. Explain to the children that they will be using the ingredients to make a bunny. Ask them what parts of the bunny they think the different ingredients might be used for.
5. Work with a small group of children to construct individual bunnies.
6. On a small plate, place one half of a canned pear with its inside down on a dry leaf of lettuce.
7. At the small end of the pear, place the cherry for a nose. Then use almonds for feet, celery for ears, raisins for eyes, and cottage cheese for the tail.
8. Add carrot sticks for the bunny to munch on.
9. When all the children have finished, they may eat their bunnies.

Questions You Can Ask

- *What was our rhyme about? What words or sounds do you remember from the rhyme?*
- *What do you remember about the book(s) we read?*
- *How did you make the bunny? What materials did you use? What did you do first, second, next, and last?*
- *What other ingredients could you use to make a bunny?*
- *What other animals could you make with these ingredients?*
- *Do you think food tastes better when you make it yourself?*

More You Can Try

- Have the children dance the bunny hop.
- Make bunny-ear hats with headbands and construction paper.

SCIENCE/LITERACY

Orange You Happy?

Words You Can Use

color, different, fruit, same, senses, texture, taste, vegetable

What You Need

- *Eating the Alphabet: Fruits and Vegetables from A to Z* by Lois Ehlert
- *The ABCs of Fruits and Vegetables and Beyond: Delicious Alphabet Poems Plus Food, Facts, and Fun for Everyone* by Steve Charney and David Goldbeck
- two of each orange fruits and vegetables, such as oranges, mangoes, peaches, tangerines, apricots, cantaloupe, carrots, butternut squash, orange tomatoes
- knife (for teacher use only)
- small plates
- napkins
- blindfolds

What You Do

Use Sound Play to gain children's interest and introduce sounds and words. Explore the vocabulary and topic further by reading one or both of the Reading Experience books. Then use the story to move into the Science Activity.

Sound Play

Repeat this tongue twister with the children three times:

Fresh fruit feeds families fast.

Reading Experience

- *Eating the Alphabet: Fruits and Vegetables from A to Z* by Lois Ehlert
- *The ABCs of Fruits and Vegetables and Beyond: Delicious Alphabet Poems Plus Food, Facts, and Fun for Everyone* by Steve Charney and David Goldbeck

Science Activity

1. Be sure to follow all safety measures (see chapter 2).
2. Select pairs of no more than five different items. If you are introducing these food concepts for the first time, explore only fruit or only vegetables until children are very familiar with all the items.
3. Leave one of each item whole. Discuss its shape. Have children draw pictures of the whole item they find the most interesting.

more →

4. In front of the children, cut the other item from each pair into small pieces. Talk about the texture inside and outside, the seeds, the smell, and so on.
5. Compare the cut pieces to the whole item.
6. Compare the foods by looking, smelling, and tasting. How are they the same? How are they different? What are their names? Do some look more alike than others? Capture the children's responses in writing as appropriate.
7. See if the children can identify the food by smelling or tasting it while wearing blindfolds.
8. Match the samples to the whole item.

Questions You Can Ask

- *What was our tongue twister about? What words or sounds do you remember from the tongue twister?*
- *What do you remember about the books we read?*
- *What are the names of each of these foods?*
- *Tell me about the outside of [name of fruit or vegetable]. What do you see?*
- *How are two [name of fruit or vegetable] the same? How are they different?*
- *What do you think will be on the inside when we cut it open?*
- *What did you think when you saw the inside? Were you surprised?*
- *Are some more alike than others?*

More You Can Try

- Create an "orange smile" by placing two slices of oranges together on a flat surface in the shape of lips. Add mini marshmallows for teeth.
- Invite children to use a hand juicer to make orange juice or lemonade.

SCIENCE/LITERACY

Kabob Pattern Cuties

Words You Can Use

graph, kabob, pattern

What You Need

- one or more books listed in the Reading Experience below
- three different kinds of fruit, such as apples, bananas, melons, strawberries, oranges, pears
- lemon juice
- plastic knife
- cutting board
- small bowls
- wooden skewers or toothpicks
- colored blocks
- index cards

What You Do

Use Sound Play to gain children's interest and introduce sounds and words. Explore the vocabulary and topic further by reading one or more of the Reading Experience books. Then use the story to move into the Science Activity.

Sound Play

Demonstrate the traditional patterns for the children and then have them make the patterns' sounds and movements. If desired, create variations and additional patterns using other physical movements and sounds.

ABAB pattern, such as clap, stomp, clap, stomp (extend by repeating)

ABBA pattern, such as clap, stomp, stomp, clap (extend by repeating)

ABC pattern, such as clap, stomp, "Ha!" (extend by repeating)

Reading Experience

- *Pattern Fish* by Trudy Harris
- *Busy Bugs: A Book about Patterns* by Jayne Harvey
- *Patterns* by Craig Hammersmith
- *Patterns Everywhere* by Julie Dalton

Science Activity

1. Be sure to follow all safety measures (see chapter 2).
2. Using colored blocks, practice making different kinds of patterns, such as ABAB, ABBA, AABB, and ABC.
3. Introduce the washed fruit. Ask the children to name the three fruits.
4. Work with the children to carefully cut up the fruit into one-half-inch pieces. Place each type of fruit in a separate bowl with a name card. Sprinkle some lemon juice over the apples to keep them from turning brown.
5. Be sure to discuss the fruits' properties, such as their textures, smells, and number of seeds.

more →

6. Introduce the skewers and invite the children to create a fruit pattern or fruit kabob using one of the patterns they have practiced. If you use toothpicks, plan on each toothpick being a pattern in part of a series. For example, using three toothpicks, the first toothpick would hold fruit in pattern AABB, the second in pattern AABB, and the third in pattern AABB. This way the child has a long series to repeat.
7. Create a fruit kabob graph and ask the children to vote on their favorite fruit to determine the class favorite.

Questions You Can Ask

- *How did we move our hands and feet? What sounds did they make? What patterns do you remember making?*
- *What do you remember about the book(s) we read?*
- *If you were going to teach your baby brother or sister to do this, how would you start? Would one of our patterns be easier than another for a younger child?*
- *How did you figure out how to keep repeating the pattern?*
- *What fruit was easiest to use? Hardest? Why?*

More You Can Try

- Have children record their patterns by drawing them on a sheet of paper.
- Create a fruit dip from one-half cup of sour cream, one teaspoon of honey, and three tablespoons of coconut.

SCIENCE/LITERACY

The Edible Aquarium

Words You Can Use

edible, float, sink

What You Need

- one or more books listed in the Reading Experience below
- a water table
- three classroom items that float and three that sink
- two large packages of blueberry-flavored gelatin
- gummy fish
- hot water
- plastic bowl
- measuring spoons
- measuring cup
- clear glass cups for gelatin
- ice cubes

What You Do

Use Sound Play to gain children's interest and introduce sounds and words. Explore the vocabulary and topic further by reading one or more of the Reading Experience books. Then use the story to move into the Science Activity.

Sound Play

Swimmy, Get Thinner

Swimmy, Swimmy, circling 'round.
Swimmy up!
Swimmy down!

Swimmy, Swimmy, doin' a crawl.
Swimmy backwards,
Saying, "Hi, ya'll!"

Swimmy, Swimmy, partner please.
Circling 'round,
Swimmy on knees.

Swimmy, Swimmy, time to hide!
Swimmy run!
Do not glide!

Swimmy, Swimmy, suck your tummy thinner,
Shark coming.
Don't be dinner!

Reading Experience

- *One Fish, Two Fish, Red Fish, Blue Fish* by Dr. Seuss
- *Rainbow Fish Opposites* by Marcus Pfister
- *Swimmy* by Leo Lionni
- *Fish Is Fish* by Leo Lionni
- *Float and Sink* by Robin Nelson
- *Flotar Y Hundirse* by Robin Nelson

Science Activity

1. Be sure to follow all safety measures (see chapter 2).
2. Practice the concepts of sinking and floating in the water table. Gather three classroom items that float and three that sink. At the water table, ask children to predict

more →

which items will float and which items will sink. Demonstrate by dropping the items into the water to see what happens.

3. Demonstrate what happens to the gummy fish when they are dropped into a glass of water.
4. Tell children they will create an edible aquarium that will help the gummy fish float.
5. Have each child pour three tablespoons of blueberry-flavored gelatin into a clear plastic cup.
6. Pour in one-half cup of hot water and stir until the gelatin dissolves. If children are young and not skilled at pouring, you should pour the hot water.
7. Let the children add two ice cubes and stir until the ice has melted and the mixture has thickened slightly.
8. If the mixture is still thin, refrigerate it until it has thickened slightly.
9. Let the children suspend gummy fish in the gelatin cups.
10. Refrigerate until set, about one hour.
11. Invite the children to watch the gummy fish "swim" in the gelatin, and eat away!

Questions You Can Ask

- *What was our poem about? What words or sounds do you remember from the poem?*
- *What do you remember about the book(s) we read?*
- *What happens when something sinks? When it floats?*
- *What do you think will happen when you drop the gummy fish into the water?*
- *What do you think will happen when you put the gummy fish into the gelatin?*

More You Can Try

- Create a "Sink or Float" chart that can be placed on a table. Ask children to place objects in the "Sink" and "Float" columns on the chart before they test the objects. Take a photo. Ask children to place objects on the chart after they test them. Take a second photo and compare. You may also simply label a chart with pictures and words to display on a wall.
- Have children draw pictures illustrating the changes in the gummy fish.
- Place one or two gummy fish in a clear container. Fill the container with water. Have the children predict what will happen if you leave the fish in the water overnight. Write down their predictions. Leave the fish in the water overnight and have the children observe the container in the morning. Discuss their observations and predictions.

SCIENCE/LITERACY

Celery Race Cars

Words You Can Use

engine, first, last, race, second, third, wheels

What You Need

- one or more books listed in the Reading Experience below
- celery sticks
- peanut butter or cream cheese
- carrot rounds
- grapes
- small plates
- tongue depressors or craft sticks
- plastic spoons
- toothpicks
- paper towels

What You Do

Use Sound Play to gain children's interest and introduce sounds and words. Explore the vocabulary and topic further by reading one or more of the Reading Experience books. Then use the story to move into the Science Activity.

Sound Play

Sing this song with the children to the tune of "She'll Be Coming 'Round the Mountain."

They'll Be Comin' 'Round the Race Track

They'll be comin' 'round the race track when they come! Beep! Beep!

They'll be comin' 'round the race track when they come!

They'll be zooming past each other

And waving to their mother.

They'll be comin' 'round the race track when they come!

Beep! Beep! Zoom! Zoom!

Reading Experience

- *Can You See What I See? Trucks and Cars* by Walter Wick
- *I Spy Little Wheels* by Jean Marzollo
- *Race Car* by Meg Parsont and Anna Curti

Science Activity

1. Be sure to follow all safety measures (see chapter 2). Be aware of any children who might be allergic to any of the food items introduced in this activity, such as peanut butter.

more →

2. Introduce the activity by showing some small toy cars and letting the children use them to race.
3. Examine the celery with the children as you wash and clean it, pulling the strings off and cutting off the stems.
4. Cut celery in four-inch sticks.
5. Provide a celery stick and small plate to each child.
6. Invite children to add one or two spoonfuls of peanut butter or cream cheese to their celery sticks, spreading it until it fills the celery sticks.
7. Use carrot rounds for the wheels and a grape for the driver's head.
8. Have the children eat their race-car creations.

Questions You Can Ask

- *What was our song about? What words or sounds do you remember from the song?*
- *What do you remember about the book(s) we read?*
- *What foods and other materials did you use to make the race cars?*
- *How did you put the race cars together? What did you do first? Second? Third? Next? Last?*
- *What other foods could we use to put inside the race car?*

More You Can Try

- Add red food coloring to one glass of water and blue food coloring to another. Set celery sticks in each glass. Ask the children to predict what might happen. Record what happens.

SCIENCE/LITERACY

Foody Friends and Boo-Noo-Noos!

Words You Can Use

apple corer, banana, crossways, peel

What You Need

- *Anna Banana and Me* by Lenore Blegvad
- *Ana Banana y Yo* by Lenore Blegvad
- one-half banana for each child
- five to six apples (approximately one horizontal round slice for each child)
- multicolored mini marshmallows
- small box raisins
- circle-shaped cereal
- peanut butter
- one vanilla wafer for each child
- one miniature peanut-butter cup for each child
- small plates
- plastic knives
- apple corer
- apple slicer
- paper towels

What You Do

Use Sound Play to gain children's interest and introduce sounds and words. Explore the vocabulary and topic further by reading one or both of the Reading Experience books. Then use the story to move into the Science Activity.

Sound Play

Apples and Bananas

I like to eat, eat, eat apples and bananas.
I like to eat, eat, eat apples and bananas.

I like to ate, ate, ate aypples and bay-nay-nays.
I like to ate, ate, ate aypples and bay-nay-nays.

I like to eet, eet, eet ee-ples and bee-nee-nees.
I like to eet, eet, eet ee-ples and bee-nee-nees.

I like to ite, ite, ite i-ples and by-by-nys.
I like to ite, ite, ite i-ples and by-by-nys.

I like to ote, ote, ote oh-ples and bo-no-nos.
I like to ote, ote, ote oh-ples and bo-no-nos.

I like to ute, ute, ute upples and bunnunus.
I like to ute, ute, ute upples and bunnunus.

Now we're through, through, through, through.
Now we're through with the apples and bananas.

Now we're through, through, through, through,
With A, E, I, O, and U.

more →

Reading Experience

- *Anna Banana and Me* by Lenore Blegvad
- *Ana Banana y Yo* by Lenore Blegvad

Science Activity

1. Be sure to follow all safety measures (see chapter 2). Be aware of any children who might be allergic to any of the food items introduced in this activity, such as peanut butter.
2. Prepare ahead by washing the apples and coring and slicing horizontally into rounds all but one apple, which will be used for demonstration.
3. Organize the banana halves, apple slices, marshmallows, raisins, cereal, vanilla wafers, and peanut-butter cups in individual bowls.
4. Put a small amount of peanut butter on a small plate for each child.
5. Demonstrate how to core and slice an apple crossways to make apple circles.
6. Give each child an apple slice to lay on his small plate.
7. Cut bananas in half. **Note**: Make sure the cut is straight so that the banana will stand up. Give one banana half to each child and have the children carefully peel the bananas.
8. Demonstrate how to use the peanut butter as glue to connect the banana to the apple base. Children should then put peanut butter in the center of their apple slices to hold the bananas in a standing position.
9. Continue to help the children use the peanut butter as glue to add cereal ears, a marshmallow nose, raisin eyes, and a vanilla-wafer hat brim with a peanut-butter cup crown.
10. As the children finish making their creations and enjoy eating them, ask questions and capture the children's responses in writing as appropriate.

Questions You Can Ask

- *What was our rhyme about? What words or sounds do you remember from the rhyme?*
- *What do you remember about the books we read?*
- *Tell me about your creation. How did you put it together?*
- *What did you use to make all the parts stick together?*
- *Did you give your creation a name?*
- *What part did you eat first? Next?*

More You Can Try

- Encourage children to use materials to make other "foody friends."
- Use apple slice instead of chocolate for top of hat.
- For small children, eliminate the face and peanut butter cup and let them stack just the apple, banana, and wafer.

SCIENCE/LITERACY

Banana-Tree Delish

Words You Can Use

center, cubed, pineapple ring, separate

What You Need

- *Chicka Chicka Boom Boom* by Bill Martin, Jr. and John Archambault
- one-half banana for each child
- one pineapple ring for each child
- one head lettuce
- small chunks of fruit, such as grapes, cherries, strawberries, other berries, peaches, pears, apples
- three or four cheese cubes for each child
- small plates
- toothpicks
- napkins

What You Do

Use Sound Play to gain children's interest and introduce sounds and words. Explore the vocabulary and topic further by reading the Reading Experience book. Then use the story to move into the Science Activity.

Sound Play

Chicka, Chicka with Attitude

Chicka, Chicka, Chicka, Chicka. (Swish palms across each other to the rhythm.)

Boom, Boom, Boom. (Stomp feet heavily for each boom.)

Repeat with same movements.

Chicka, Chicka, Chicka, Chicka. (Swish hands across hips to the rhythm.)

Boom, Boom, Boom. (Clap heavily for each boom.)

Repeat with same movements.

Turn and Touch, Turn and Touch. (Children turn around and touch the floor with their hands.)

Stop. (Freeze.)

Sit. (Sit.)

Reading Experience

- *Chicka Chicka Boom Boom* by Bill Martin, Jr. and John Archambault

Science Activity

1. Be sure to follow all safety measures (see chapter 2).
2. Prepare cubed cheese and fruit pieces and organize all materials in bowls in advance.
3. Wash and dry the lettuce, and separate the leaves. You may have children help you.
4. Give each child a small plate to use to construct her banana "tree." The first layer is a leaf of lettuce, followed by a pineapple ring.
5. Have each child insert a banana half into the pineapple ring. Assist the children if necessary.

more →

6. Children can decorate their banana trees using toothpicks to place small fruit chunks and cheese cubes as "branches" on the banana trees. Provide five to seven pieces for each child.
7. Encourage children to identify the foods they use as they add branches to their trees.
8. Eat and enjoy!

Questions You Can Ask

- *What was our rhyme about? What words or sounds do you remember from the rhyme?*
- *What do you remember about the book we read?*
- *How did you build your banana tree? What foods did you use?*
- *What did you do first? Second? Third? Next? Last?*
- *What was the most difficult part?*

More You Can Try

- Compare and contrast the banana tree with the activity in Foody Friends and Boo-Noo-Noos!
- Have children draw apple and banana people or animals, and dictate or write a story about them.
- Have children keep a group record of how many fruit chunks and how many cheese cubes they use to create their banana trees.

SCIENCE/LITERACY

Slithering Banana Boa—Sssssssssssss

Words You Can Use

boa, slither

What You Need

- *The Day Jimmy's Boa Ate the Wash* by Trinka Hakes Noble
- *Jimmy's Boa and the Big Splash Birthday Bash* by Trinka Hakes Noble
- one banana for each child
- one head lettuce
- five carrots
- peanut butter
- chow mein noodles
- raisins
- bread crumbs
- small candies
- small plates
- plastic knives
- carrot peeler
- paper towels

What You Do

Use Sound Play to gain children's interest and introduce sounds and words. Explore the vocabulary and topic further by reading one or both of the Reading Experience books. Then use the story to move into the Science Activity.

Sound Play

Tell children to touch their body parts as they are described in this poem.

Slithering Sally–A Boa Story

Slithering Sally slides up.
I wish I were in a dream, I scream!

Slithering Sally slides up.
She curls around my arm, I'm alarmed!

Slithering Sally slides up.
Her tongue flicks my toes, oh no!

Slithering Sally slides up.
A kid tries to give me a kiss, she gives a hiss!

Slithering Sally slides up.
Do boas know how to grin? Is she my friend?

Slithering Sally slides up.
This time I don't feel a scream, we're a team!

Reading Experience

- *The Day Jimmy's Boa Ate the Wash* by Trinka Hakes Noble
- *Jimmy's Boa and the Big Splash Birthday Bash* by Trinka Hakes Noble

more →

Science Activity

1. Be sure to follow all safety measures (see chapter 2).
2. Create a rebus recipe for the children.
3. Wash the carrots and lettuce. Dry the lettuce and separate its leaves.
4. Review the rebus recipe with the children.
5. Children can tear up lettuce leaves into small pieces and put them on the plates for grass.
6. Assist children in peeling a banana and slicing it into round sections. Set aside the ends of the banana for the head and tail of the snake.
7. Dab peanut butter on both ends of the banana slices and place them in a row on a plate. Add the small banana ends for the head and tail.
8. Children may decorate the peanut-butter parts with chow mein noodles, raisins, bread crumbs, and/or small candies. Encourage them to use materials creatively. Provide each child with a carrot peel for the snake's tongue.
9. Ask children questions and capture their responses in writing as they eat their snake snacks.

Questions You Can Ask

- *What was our poem about? What words or sounds do you remember from the poem?*
- *What do you remember about the book(s) we read?*
- *Tell me about your slithering snake. What did you do to create such an interesting boa constrictor?*
- *How can you move and sound like a snake? Show me how your snake moves and makes snake noises.*

More You Can Try

- Use unifix cubes to create snakes using patterns.
- Have children tell stories about how they are going to eat their boa constrictors.
- Cut twelve-inch lengths of adding-machine tape and one-inch squares of colored construction paper. Children can glue the construction squares in a pattern on the tape.

SCIENCE/LITERACY

Any Which Way—It's an Apple!

Words You Can Use

crunch, peel, sweet, tart

What You Need

- one or more of the books listed in the Reading Experience below
- three each of five different kinds of apples with different colors and tastes, such as Red Delicious, Granny Smith, Golden Delicious, Fiji, Gala
- baskets
- chart paper
- apple corer/slicer
- plastic knife
- apple peeler
- potato peeler
- small plates
- paper towels
- kitchen scale
- balance scale
- various classroom items, such as buttons and rocks

What You Do

Use Sound Play to gain children's interest and introduce sounds and words. Explore the vocabulary and topic further by reading one or more of the Reading Experience books. Then use the story to move into the Science Activity.

Sound Play

Recite "Way Up High in the Apple Tree" in English and then in Spanish.

Make five apples out of red or green felt and use Velcro fasteners to attach them to a song card you've made showing a picture of an apple tree. Start with five apples on the picture and have the children count them. Sing the song, and ask a child to take off one apple for each verse. Ask, "How many apples are left?" (or in Spanish: "¿Quantas manzanas quedad?") each time a child removes an apple.

Way Up High in the Apple Tree/Bien alto en el árbol de manzanas

Way up high in the apple tree,
Five little apples smiled at me.
So I shook that tree as gently as I could,
One fell down and, mmmm, it was good!

Bien alto en el árbol de manzanas,
Cinco manzanitas sonreían a mi,
Sacudí el árbol muy fuerte así,
Una se cayó, mmmm, que rico para mí.

Repeat the verse, each time replacing "Five" or "Cinco" with the appropriate number (Four/Cuatro, Three/Tres, Two/Dos, One/Uno).

Reading Experience

- *Apples* by Gail Gibbons
- *Our Apple Tree* by Gorel Kristina Naslund
- *One Green Apple* by Eve Bunting

more →

- *The Seasons of Arnold's Apple Tree* by Gail Gibbons
- *Apples* by Inez Snyder
- *Apples, Apples* by Salina Yoon
- *Apples, Apples* by Kathleen Weidner Zoehfeld

Science Activity

1. Be sure to follow all safety measures (see chapter 2).
2. Wash the apples in advance. Place a variety of the apples in several baskets.
3. Create a KWL chart on chart paper. This is a chart with three columns: K = What do I Know about apples? W = What do I Want to know about apples? L = What did I Learn about apples?
4. Gather the children before the KWL chart. Ask what they know and want to know about apples, and write their answers in the K and W chart columns.
5. With the children, explore and examine the outside of each of the types of apples.
6. Explore the apples' weights using a kitchen scale to look at and record a numeral. Use a balance scale to compare. Use the terms *more* and *less* with other apples and with other classroom items such as buttons or rocks.
7. Graph apples by color.
8. Using a corer/slicer, core and cut the apples into sections. Cut each section into quarters. Let children examine and explore the texture, color, smell, and taste of the apples. On a second piece of chart paper, write down words that children use to describe the apples. Ask them to think about which one might be the sweetest, most tart, and crunchiest, and record this information on a second chart.
9. Demonstrate how children can use an apple peeler/corer to remove the peel in one piece and remove the core. Demonstrate how to use a potato peeler to remove a peel.
10. Encourage children to try the different peelers, and use a string to record their longest lengths of peel. They may need to work in pairs. Let the children compare peel lengths.
11. Share the *Apple Star* story (www.mrsmcgowan.com/1stgrade/applestory.htm) with the children. Demonstrate how to cut the apple crosswise to discover the star and to make apple rounds. Examine each type of apple to see whether they all have stars.
12. After apple exploration, have children taste and eat the apples.

Questions You Can Ask

- *What was our song about? What words or sounds do you remember from the song?*
- *What do you remember about the book(s) we read?*
- *What different ways did you use to take the peel off the apples?*
- *How do the apples sound in your mouth? How do the apples taste?*
- *Describe how you would know an apple is tart.*

More You Can Try

- Make apple prints with the "star." Press the apple into a paint-soaked sponge and use it as a stamp on paper.

SCIENCE/LITERACY

Growing Jack's Beanstalk

Words You Can Use

chlorophyll, dry, gardening, growth, leaves, light, moist, roots, seeds, soaking, stem

What You Need

- one or more of the books listed in the Reading Experience below
- lima beans
- snack-sized paper towels
- resealable plastic bags
- stapler
- water

What You Do

Use Sound Play to gain children's interest and introduce sounds and words. Explore the vocabulary and topic further by reading one or more of the Reading Experience books. Then use the story to move into the Science Activity.

Sound Play

When Jack's a Very Good Boy

When Jack's a very good boy,
He shall have cakes and custard.
But when he does nothing but cry,
He shall have nothing but mustard.

Reading Experience

- *Jack and the Beanstalk* retold by Paul Galdone
- *Jack and the Beanstalk* retold by Steven Kellogg
- *Ten Seeds* by Ruth Brown
- *Giants Have Feelings, Too/Jack and the Beanstalk* by Alvin Granowsky
- *Jack and the Beanstalk* retold by John Kurtz
- *The Tiny Seed* by Eric Carle
- *Curious George Plants a Seed* adaptation by Erica Zappy

Science Activity

1. Show the children the parts of a plant (root, stem, leaves) and talk about the growing process.
2. Use creative dramatics to encourage the children to act out the growth of the beanstalk from a seed putting down roots, slowly growing the stalk, and developing leaves.
3. Have the children wet a snack-sized paper towel, squeeze out the excess water, and carefully place it in a resealable plastic bag.
4. Add two or three lima beans spaced apart in the paper towel.
5. Hang the bags on a bulletin board that receives a lot of sunlight.
6. Notice and record the changes.
7. Cook and taste some lima beans. Talk about the beans' relation to those you "planted" in the bags.

more →

Questions You Can Ask

- *What was our rhyme about? What words or sounds do you remember from the rhyme?*
- *What do you remember about the book(s) we read?*
- *What is happening to the beans?*
- *What do these beans need to grow?*
- *What other kinds of beans or seeds do you eat?*

More You Can Try

Invite families to go on a seed hunt in their kitchen to find other seeds, such as popcorn kernels, apple seeds, orange seeds, avocadoes, and so on. Families and children can label and send the seeds to school.

Appendix A

REBUS RECIPE ART

Boo-noo-noos and Friends

Make photocopies of this page to use with "Foody Friends and Boo-Noo-Noos!" on page 221.

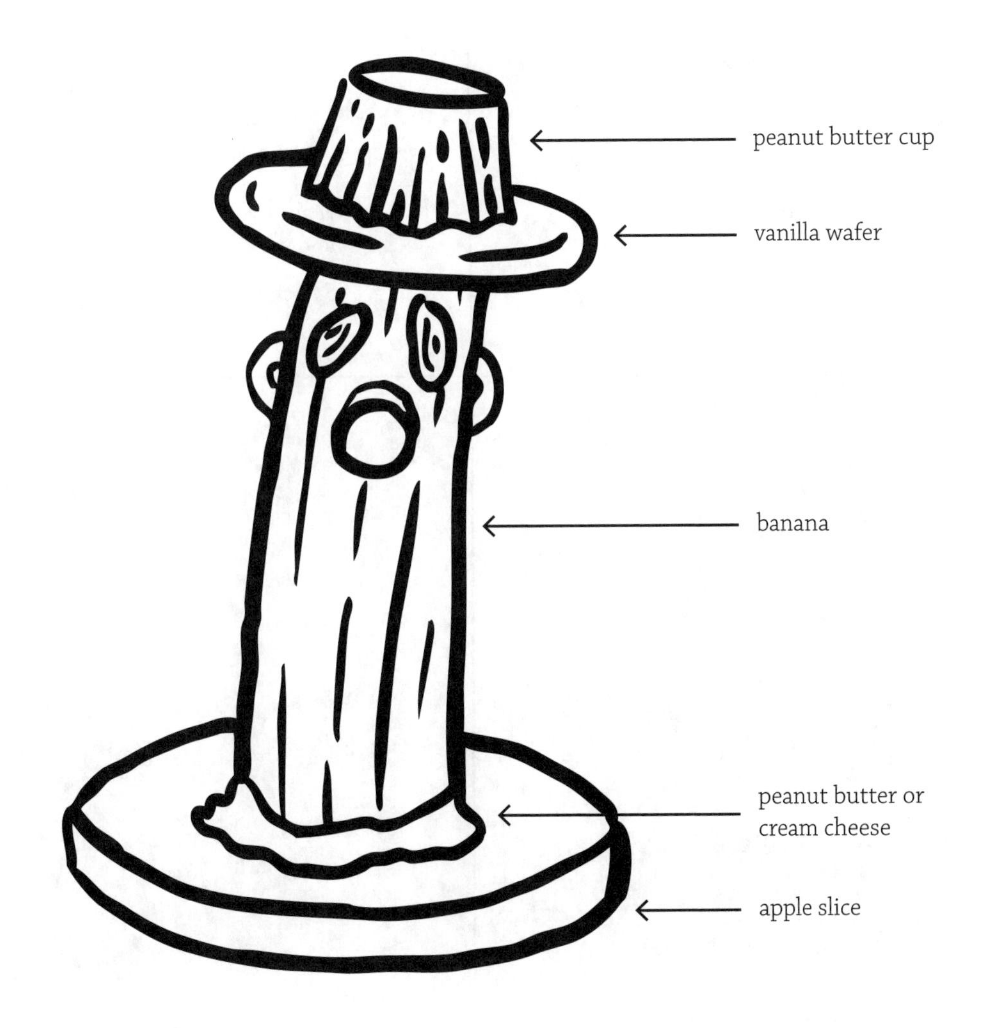

Gingerbread Man

Make photocopies of this page to use with "Catch Me If You Can!" on page 193.

1

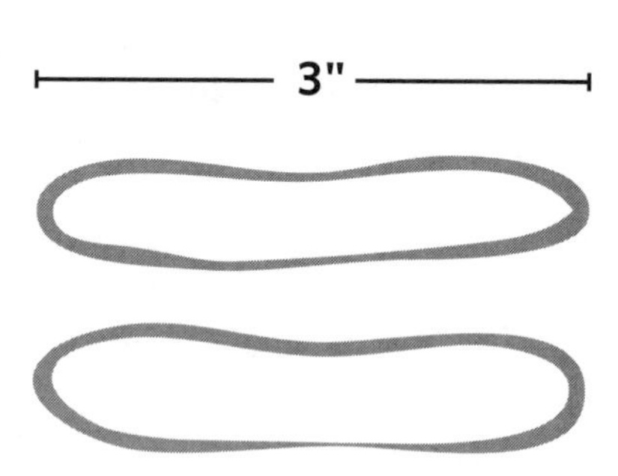

- Make two snakes about 3" long.
- Make an extra one if you want to make a gingerbread girl.

2

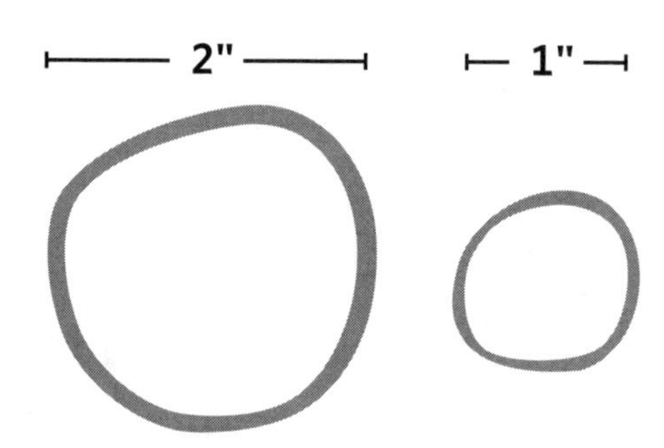

- Make two balls: one 2" in diameter and one 1" in diameter.
- Smash them flat.

3

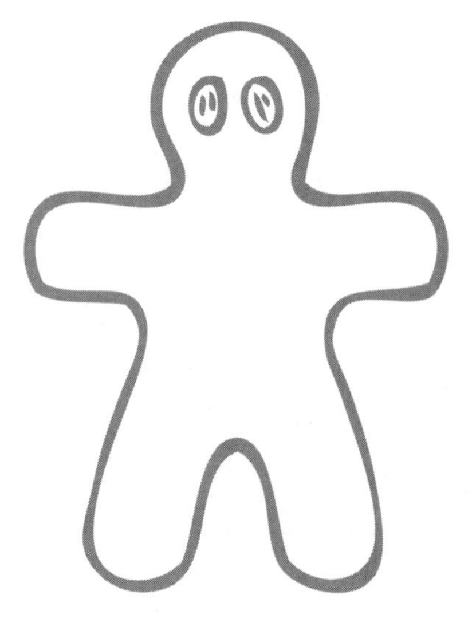

- Make a gingerbread boy!
- Add raisin eyes.

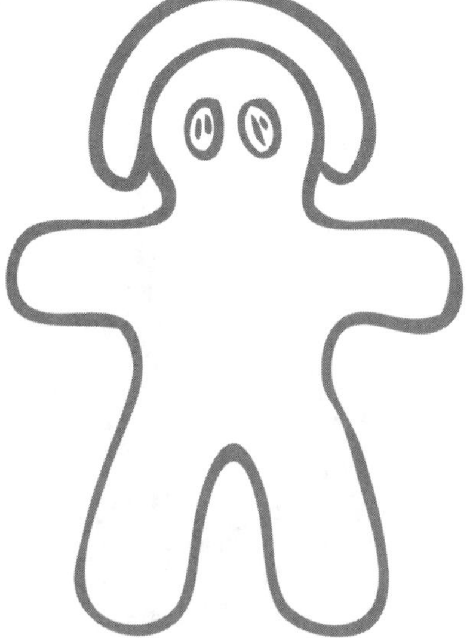

- Make a gingerbread girl!
- Add raisin eyes.

Pancakes for One

Make photocopies of this page to use with "Pancakes and Flapjacks!" on page 209.

1

- Beat eggs in advance.
- Put aside.

2

- Add two tablespoons of baking mix.

3

- Add two tablespoons of milk.

4

- Add one teaspoon of beaten eggs.

5

- Stir. Sing "Happy Birthday" one time.

6

- Apply cooking oil or spray and heat the skillet.
- Pour batter onto the skillet.
- Cook and turn.

7

One Child: One Pudding

Make photocopies of this page to use with "Rice Is Nice, Eat It Twice!" on page 183.

1

- Put two tablespoons of instant pudding into a bowl or cup.

2

- Add two tablespoons of dry milk and stir.

3

- Add ⅓ cup of water.

4

- Stir for two minutes (sing "Happy Birthday" four times).

5

- Cool in a refrigerator.

6

- Add two tablespoons of cooked rice, stir, and eat.

Appendix B

SCIENCE PROCESS AND SKILLS ALIGNMENT CHART FOR CHAPTER 3 ACTIVITIES

ACTIVITY	OBSERVING/SIGHT	OBSERVING/SMELL	OBSERVING/TASTE	OBSERVING/TOUCH	OBSERVING/SOUND	CLASSIFYING	COMMUNICATING	MEASURING	INFERRING	PREDICTING
Look and See	■									
Which Lemon Is Mine?	■									
Sha Zam! Food Changes Form!	■									
Flavored Gelatin: Sink or Float?	■									
Can You Guess the Color?	■									
Pea Puddles	■									
Coconut Crazy	■									
Sugar Rainbow	■									
Baggie Bread	■									
Pretty Penny	■									
Egg-Carton Rainbows	■									
Cucumber Magic	■									
Can You Guess the Odor?		■								
Can You Know without the Nose?		■								
Matching Odors		■								
Does It Smell or Not?		■								
Sniff Identification		■								
Shoe Box of Scents		■								
Sniff Walk		■								

ACTIVITY	OBSERVING/SIGHT	OBSERVING/SMELL	OBSERVING/TASTE	OBSERVING/TOUCH	OBSERVING/SOUND	CLASSIFYING	COMMUNICATING	MEASURING	INFERRING	PREDICTING
Smelly Stickers		■								
Smelly Jelly Beans		■								
Look Alike but Smell Different		■								
Look Different but Smell Alike		■								
Can You Tell the Smell?		■								
Creating Fun Smell Cards		■								
Please Smell the Gifts!		■								
Flavorless Gum		■								
Vegetable Texture Tasting			■							
Taste Look-Alikes			■							
Classifying Tastes			■							
Fruit-Salad Sensations			■							
Pickle Pucker Pick			■							
Salt or Sugar?			■							
Bread Around the World			■							
Taste Tests			■							
Tasting Party			■							
Smorgasbord Soup			■							
Taster's Choice			■							
White Taste Test			■							
Fee, Fi, Fo, Fum—What Am I Feeling with My Thumbs?				■						
Feet Are Neat! What's Under the Sheet?				■						
Exotic Fruits				■						
Salted or Unsalted?				■						
Shish Kabobs				■						
This Is So Cool!				■						

ACTIVITY	OBSERVING/SIGHT	OBSERVING/SMELL	OBSERVING/TASTE	OBSERVING/TOUCH	OBSERVING/SOUND	CLASSIFYING	COMMUNICATING	MEASURING	INFERRING	PREDICTING
You're All Wet!				■						
Digging for Copper				■						
Some Like It Hot, Some Like It Cold!				■						
Rough and Smooth				■						
Fine and Coarse				■						
Guess the Sound					■					
Having a Band Blast!					■					
What Am I Opening?					■					
Pumpkin Pitch					■					
What Do You Hear?					■					
Matching Sounds					■					
Can-Can Jingles					■					
Dropping In					■					
Will It Sink or Float?						■				
Classifying Taste						■				
Mixed-Up Madness						■				
Looking at Licorice						■				
Rainbow Sort						■				
Candy-Worm Wiggle						■				
Counting Candy						■				
Isn't This Cool?						■				
Sorting Seeds						■				
Frozen-Food Frenzy						■				
Cookie Caper						■				
This Is Really Cool!						■				
Fruit-Kabob Rainbow						■				

ACTIVITY	OBSERVING/SIGHT	OBSERVING/SMELL	OBSERVING/TASTE	OBSERVING/TOUCH	OBSERVING/SOUND	CLASSIFYING	COMMUNICATING	MEASURING	INFERRING	PREDICTING
Soak 'Em						■				
I've Been Changed!						■				
Make No Beans about It!						■				
Favorite Juice							■			
Write It Down							■			
No Words Allowed							■			
Are You "Raisinably" Sure?							■			
Flavor Burst							■			
Cut and See							■			
Question of the Day							■			
What's in the Bag?							■			
Fruit and Seed Sculptures							■			
Tinkering with Tools							■			
Chocolate-Chip Cookie Communications							■			
Advertising Apples							■			
Soak It Up!								■		
How Much Will It Hold?								■		
Which Is the Heaviest of Them All?								■		
Can You "Bear" It?								■		
Measuring with Cotton Swabs								■		
Jelly Bean Balancing								■		
Lengths of Licorice								■		
Chocolate and Marshmallow Measuring								■		
Candy-Dust Discovery								■		
Baby Bagels								■		
Pancake Patties								■		

ACTIVITY	OBSERVING/SIGHT	OBSERVING/SMELL	OBSERVING/TASTE	OBSERVING/TOUCH	OBSERVING/SOUND	CLASSIFYING	COMMUNICATING	MEASURING	INFERRING	PREDICTING
French-Fry Frenzy								■		
Sweet as Sugar									■	
Mystery Bag									■	
Salt and Pepper Mix-Up									■	
Impressions									■	
Foil Cover-Up									■	
Foot Feely Center									■	
Dancing Raisins									■	
Celery Soak									■	
Make No Bones About It!									■	
Pea Power									■	
Rubber Eggs									■	
Runaway Droplets										■
Swelling Raisins										■
Freeze!										■
Colored-Candy Predicting										■
Animal-Cracker Predicting										■
Exactly What Color?										■
Cereal Skewers										■
Pizza Pizzazz										■
Fruit and Vegetables: Sink or Float?										■
Carton and Container Predicting										■
Popcorn Predicting										■
Candy Counts										■

Appendix C

SCIENCE PROCESS AND MATH SKILLS ALIGNMENT CHART FOR CHAPTER 4 ACTIVITIES

This chart aligns the activities with science and math skills. It identifies the science process skills as described earlier in this book and supported by the National Science Foundation. As an additional bonus, math skills as supported by the research and recommendations of the National Council of Teachers of Mathematics (NCTM) have been included to further identify the value of these activities to curriculum goals and positive outcomes for children.

ACTIVITY	SCIENCE/OBSERVATION	SCIENCE/CLASSIFICATION	SCIENCE/MEASUREMENT	SCIENCE/COMMUNICATION	SCIENCE/INFERENCE	SCIENCE/PREDICTION	MATH/NUMBER AND OBSERVATION	MATH/PATTERNS	MATH/GEOMETRY AND SPACIAL SENSE	MATH/MEASUREMENT	MATH/CLASSIFICATION AND DATA COLLECTION
Good-for-You Food	■	■		■	■				■		■
It's a Neat Feat to Eat Wheat!	■	■		■		■	■			■	■
"Just for Me!" Bread	■		■	■						■	
Hen Pickin's	■		■	■			■			■	
Art Toast	■			■	■	■			■		
Roasted Toast	■			■	■	■			■		■
Roll 'Em Up	■			■	■	■			■		■
Iron a Sandwich	■			■	■	■			■		
Rice Is Nice, Eat It Twice!	■		■	■					■	■	
Chopstick Pick-Up Cakes	■			■					■		
Rice Burgers	■		■	■		■				■	
Yummy, Messy Rice!	■		■	■					■		
Gooble and Giggle Necklace	■	■		■				■			
Catch Me If You Can!	■		■	■			■		■	■	■
Taco Food Bar	■			■			■				

ACTIVITY	SCIENCE/OBSERVATION	SCIENCE/CLASSIFICATION	SCIENCE/MEASUREMENT	SCIENCE/COMMUNICATION	SCIENCE/INFERENCE	SCIENCE/PREDICTION	MATH/NUMBER AND OBSERVATION	MATH/PATTERNS	MATH/GEOMETRY AND SPACIAL SENSE	MATH/MEASUREMENT	MATH/CLASSIFICATION AND DATA COLLECTION
Popcorn Sculpture	■			■		■			■		
Alphabet Pretzels	■		■	■					■	■	
Eating The Three Bears	■			■	■		■		■		
Bagel Exploration	■	■		■		■					■
The Three Bears' Porridge	■		■	■		■				■	■
Measure with Spaghetti	■		■	■							
Pancakes and Flapjacks	■		■	■						■	
Bunny Foo-Foo	■			■			■		■		
Orange You Happy?	■			■		■			■		
Kabob Pattern Cuties	■			■				■	■		
The Edible Aquarium	■			■	■	■					
Celery Race Cars	■			■			■		■		
Foody Friends and Boo-Noo-Noos!	■		■	■		■	■			■	■
Banana-Tree Delish	■	■		■					■		
Slithering Banana Boa—Sssssssssssss	■			■	■				■		
Any Which Way—It's an Apple!	■		■	■					■	■	
Growing Jack's Beanstalk	■			■	■	■					■

REFERENCES

Alfving, Albert M., C. Lloyd Eitzen, Joanne Hyman, Rose Lee Patron, Helen Holve, and Philip Nelson. 1987. *Fun with foods: a recipe for math + science.* Fresno, CA: AIMS Education Foundation.

Burns, Marilyn. 2007. *About teaching mathematics: A K–8 resource.* Sausalito, CA: Math Solutions Publications.

Copple, Carol, and Sue Bredekamp, eds. 2009. *Developmentally appropriate practice in early childhood programs: Serving children from birth through age 8.* 3rd ed. Washington, DC: National Association for the Education of Young Children.

Gossett, Carol, Jill Delano, Virginia Kramer, Valerie Welk, and Carol Wood. 1994. *Sense-able science.* Fresno, CA: AIMS Educational Foundation.

International Reading Association (IRA) and National Association for the Education of Young Children (NAEYC). 1998. Learning to read and write: Developmentally appropriate practices for young children. Joint position statement. Newark, DE: International Reading Association.

Johnson, Barbara, and Betty Plemons. 1998. *Cup cooking: Individual child-portion picture recipes.* Lake Alfred, FL: Early Educators Press.

Landry, Susan. 2005. *Effective early childhood programs: Turning knowledge into action.* Houston: University of Texas Houston Health Science Center.

Moore, Carolyn E., Mimi H. Kerr, and Robert J. Shulman. 1990. *Young chef's nutrition guide and cookbook.* New York: Barron's. pp. 54–55.

National Scientific Council on the Developing Child. 2004. Young children develop in an environment of relationships. Working Paper 1. Center on the Developing Child at Harvard University.

National Scientific Council on the Developing Child. 2007. The Timing and Quality of Early Experiences Combine to Shape Brain Architecture. Working Paper 5. Center on the Developing Child at Harvard University.

Schickedanz, Judith A. 1986. *More than the ABCs: The early stages of reading and writing.* Washington, DC: National Association for the Education of Young Children.

Schiller, Pam. 1999. Turning knowledge into practice. *Child Care Information Exchange.* (126): 49–52.

Stephens, K. 1999. Primed for learning: The young child's mind. *Child Care Information Exchange.* (126): 44–48.

Tomlinson, Heather Bigger, and Marilou Hyson. 2009. Developmentally appropriate practice in the preschool years—ages 3–5. In *Developmentally appropriate practice in early childhood programs serving children from birth through age 8.* 3rd ed. Edited by Carol Copple and Sue Bredekamp, 111–83. Washington, DC: National Association for the Education of Young Children.

ABOUT THE AUTHORS

Liz Plaster, MEd, is a nationally known education and business professional. Her experience as an administrator, business leader, teacher, and mentor-teacher in settings ranging from public/private schools, private businesses, Head Start, universities, junior colleges, and social service arenas has given her a variety of experiences in working with both children and adults from varied backgrounds. She is an expert in human behavior and performance.

Liz graduated from Texas Tech University with a BS in Human Science and has an MEd from the University of St. Thomas in Houston, Texas. She has been an award recipient for her contributions in the field of education, served as a National Head Start Mentor in Literacy, and worked with Susan Landry at the University of Texas Health Science Center to implement a statewide mentoring project that integrated literacy and language into all areas of the classroom.

Her interest in mentoring and coaching others led to her being certified through the International Coach Federation (ICF). Additionally, Ms. Plaster is a Certified Associate of Six Seconds, the foremost emotional intelligence training and assessment organization in the world.

Rick Krustchinsky, EdD, has been a teacher at the elementary, junior high, and university level for over thirty years. He has worked extensively in Alabama, Mississippi, and Texas. His areas of interest are elementary math and science education. He presents to professional groups and schools, serves on the advisory boards of several organizations, and is the author of numerous articles in the field of elementary math and science education. Currently Rick is a professor of education at the University of St. Thomas in Houston, Texas. As a professor, he has won awards for his teaching and service to children. He was most recently honored with the University of St. Thomas Aquinas Excellence in Teaching Award. Rick holds a BS and MEd from Stephen F. Austin State University and an EdD from the University of Southern Mississippi. He is married and the father of two children.